JOURNEYS ON
MIND MOUNTAIN

JOURNEYS ON MIND MOUNTAIN

G. BlueStone

Celestial Arts
Berkeley, California

Avant Press
P.O. Box 526
Fort Collins, Colorado 80522

Cover design by Ken Scott
Text design by Sal Glynn
Composition by Wilsted & Taylor

Library of Congress Cataloging-in-Publication Data

BlueStone, G.
　Journeys on mind mountain / G. BlueStone.
　　p.　cm.
　　ISBN 0-89087-577-4
　　1. Meditations.　2. Meditation.　I. Title.
BL627.B57　1989
158'.12—dc20
89-7052
CIP

First Printing, 1990

0　9　8　7　6　5　4　3　2　1

Manufactured in the United States of America

CONTENTS

JOURNEYS ON
MIND MOUNTAIN

INTRODUCTION

THIS COLLECTION OF JOURNEYS in the mountains and desert is a reminder of richness lost; a book intended to strike a strangely familiar chord, which is already vibrating softly, though perhaps hidden somewhere within the reader. It is a book intended to stir a remembrance that has become hazy from long disuse, a rich-textured remembrance hard to touch, to hold, like a beautiful but forgotten dream shyly hiding in the stark light of day. It is intended to prompt each individual to regain the freshness, the depth of life, which has been somehow allowed to fade like water carried too long in cupped palms, a return to the magic traditionally accorded only the sage and denied the rest. It is a collection of forays, made by the reader in an open-minded state of readiness, forays into the realm of the sages, not with any intent of theft or demand of tribute, no souvenirs to bring home—but just to see what might happen when we remember, when we hear that chord, which is already softly vibrating within. Perhaps the reader may come to an understanding more intimate than intellectual, to a big broad view transcending any viewpoint. It's all possible here. The reader who is avid for those possibilities, for something that is not small and cramped, will begin to make forays into that land beyond conditioning on his or her own. To somewhere with plenty of room to stretch.

Each journey is a journey for the whole being, involving all the senses, and in each is written a different trip, on a different day, over the course of the seasons. Each is like a Chinese landscape: nature alone predominates, the lone character is small, unobtrusive, the painter invisible, existing only in what is seen and heard. The thoughts become the reader's thoughts, lightly placed so as not to interfere. Gently inserted as if by the mind of the reader. The hard line between author and reader breaks down and with it dissolves the divisive wall between nature and intellect.

Each journey is presented in such a way that it comes alive over and over each time it is read anew. Each becomes active within the reader on two levels: each is, on the one hand, a meditation, which remains to be deepened by the reader, taken within and digested until its special quality comes to permeate the life of the reader and, on the other hand, each is an expression of subtle textures and states that, though not ends in themselves, point always back to a state of inner stillness, which must be present before the mind can apprehend them. Once read, they continue to do their work within, unaided and without strain, as a stone thrown in a deep pool continues deeper and deeper until it inevitably reaches the bottom. This is a book on breaking the surface and falling to the bottom.

It is a book on meditation, which never mentions meditation. A book on sharply honing the human spirit, which doesn't rely on method for that honing. One reads between the lines and is brought beyond that damnable question, that old obstacle called "how?" One reads, listening and watching, and is taken up by an undertone that was always there but was previously unnoticed. It is not intended that this book be studied like a text, but rather that each journey be *taken* by the reader, that each is read in the way one listens to a piece of music. Like Chinese landscapes, each chapter is a journey that requires no traveler at all. The only thing needed is an attentive mind hungry for something larger than ideas, something greater than the small mind itself. Something beyond the feeble memories of living impulses, which remain trapped and hidden within the cramped confines of the skull.

When one comes to feel the never-ending flow of time as a gentle caress, there comes a continual renewal emerging like a spring; an ever-refreshing vibrancy comes to permeate life, crumbling the rigid walls that surround the heart. For too long people have chosen to regard this sense of living fullness solely as the distant province of vague sages in lands somewhere far away. It is always here when one remembers; always here when one knows how to look clearly without stirring things up, muddying the water. It is always here right now, closer than an indrawn breath, and it is a journey each one must take for oneself.

For it is each one's responsibility to go deeper than ever before, to hear that undertone for himself, or herself, and so move easily beyond the flat world of the map of memory into the freshness of the living present.

RETURN TO SPRING

SPRING COMES LATE high up in the mountains. The higher you go, the later it arrives. If you're willing to climb, to let go of each springtime as it arises and recedes below, you can enter into that alluring freshness of new grasses and radiant wildflowers again and again until you finally reach the glaciers, the frozen fields where yesterday's snows and tomorrow's will soon meet and blend. An intersection of past and future where the streams of time melt off, dissolve, as do all things born of time, to become the cold clear glacial waters—the flowing streams of the present. The best way is to follow those streams right up to their source. Returning to the source is always the best way for a human being to go. Walk right up the cascading path of icy crystal, step from stone to hoary stone all the way to the blue-white glaciers above, up to the matrix. There is a place in the ancient topmost firs, even to the whitebark pines and above, near timberline, where spring, summer and fall all arrive and depart in September. A mile and a half below, this year's spring has come and gone some months ago.

So you wander the mountain streams up to hidden ravines and lush valleys, places that have only just become, perhaps even today, alive with color, overflowing with that fresh vibrancy that is the richness of what has been named "spring." The flowing water is frigid, born only moments before of a melting glacier. Monkeyflowers grin clownishly on the banks—banks thick with violets and monkshood, fragrant bog orchids and a score of others, which most have allowed to decay, leaving only empty names and dry pieces of knowledge. The breath of life again squeezed out by the acquiring mind. Always watch this warily; be on guard so you don't let the profound decay into the mundane. Let others sanction the mundane. *Why should you?*

The flowers dazzle with a display that is totally, completely innocent, with none of the pretense of an exhibition. There's not a sign of anyone up here. They all stick to the trails. Most will only see that which others have seen before. Look in the same manner in which others have looked before. *Why should you? Who are you anyway?* No others have seen this artless show this spring or will see it before autumn arrives in perhaps another week, before winter arrives in perhaps two. Only the squirrels chirr in the branches while raucous nutcrackers fly overhead performing flips and stalls in mid-flight.

People are always performing for others, always concerned with self-image. They may watch for the expected reaction of others, but not their own, so action becomes the insidious work of self-image feeding itself. Where there is self-consciousness there is no innocence. They carry their images like precious tonnage. How many have gone beyond? Gone beyond praise and blame, no longer caught within the prism of image, but rather unconsciously manifesting beauty and freshness naturally? How many would know what it is to drop the frozen image and let it dissolve as do the glaciers? How many would walk in the mountains and participate in spring? Even for a moment. Even for a moment you must pass beyond to innocence and freshness, and then beyond *that* innocence and freshness to those that are not mere pieces of knowledge—to *that* unstained by memory and imagination.

Then that timeless instant may stand to purify all the rest. Then you have lost yourself in it all and become a flower of the spring. Whether that spring is long or short matters not, for it is a spring filled with intensity and beauty. If it is short, then that very brevity serves to enhance and intensify. Whether it arrives in April or September doesn't really matter.

A raven is circling high above. The circles of jet black erode almost lazily into soft gray traces, which dissolve and vanish on the billowy clouds. The clouds to the west are joining together, flattening, forming thunderheads. The breeze has turned cool. Overhead a large patch of deep blue. Faraway thunder rolls through the afternoon. It passes through you, felt as much as heard.

The bold gray and white nutcrackers turn and dart in the air. They alight on a huge snowfield, cracking the seeds from the cones of the whitebark pines, highest of the trees. The incessant winds have twisted them into a thick tangle of contorted shrubs. The birds are a gregarious lot and socialize clamorously as they devour the seeds. The white snow has become littered with broken cones. Acres of pussywillows grow like a maze along the sparkling rivulets that pour and divide from the glacier. The raven has become a small black dot. Everything of the past and future is within that dot. Flying away. Becoming smaller and smaller. If you don't keep a question now the dot will become larger again. That's the way of things. Ask yourself, deeply, searchingly, about the flowers. Ask yourself for whom they bloom each spring in September?

THE APRIL MIND

What of a mind that thinks yet is not lost in thought? An uncramped mind with vast beautiful spaces to roam? Endless spaces devoid of traces past and future, wide-open ranges of the present larger than the mind itself? It's from the vastness of those open ranges that life's freshness emerges.

A branch snaps sharply in the dark and you listen. Be still and hear the thousand sounds of the night. The chorus of crickets chirping, frogs croaking insistently at the edge of a small pond. An invisible owl hooting half the night in a tall pine and the padding and scurrying of small and even smaller feet. Or the city sounds: the steady hum of traffic on the highway, the deep growls and groans of ponderous dinosaur buses and the explosive hiss of air brakes. The sounds of human nightlife, whose arrhythmic footfalls scuff and scrape the sidewalks instead of padding lightly. Listen closely, intimately, to the night sounds, and then learn to hear your thoughts each as but another sound emerging in the still of the night. Or learn to watch every thought as but another image of things that arise on a sunny April afternoon.

Spring has come of itself once more. Yet to call it "spring" is to express what cannot be expressed in words. An attempt to capture the incomprehensible on cold reels of thought.

Clean, willowy daffodils and vibrant hyacinths, appearing from out of the inexpressible, stand clear and distinct, intensely vivid in a way that can only be known after a long gray cold. The afternoon is sunny and mild, almost balmy, and it's an early spring for these parts. The fresh country air is laced with the sweet deep fragrance of the hyacinths and with the living scent of a new spring, a scent that can only be caught when the air greeting your nostrils is within a certain narrow temperature range. Neither too cold nor too hot. The hyacinths' sweet perfume floats delicately on the warm April breeze. A bumblebee buzzes around the garden, its busy drone mingling with the wind like a steady fragrance of its own. A fragrance that seems to hold in the spring air for a time without diminishing in intensity. The squeaking call of a newly arrived cowbird intersects the drone in several places, then both vanish, leaving only the sound of the wind playing the rough woodwinds of the pine branches. Blowing through the polished reeds of new green grass. *Listen*. There's always the sound of sound taking its myriad forms. *Listen*. Sometimes there is just the sound of sound.

You listen to each form in turn and sometimes to a harmony of two or three parts. When you can listen without becoming lost, you can hear in a new way. When you can listen to your thoughts without becoming lost in what you hear; when you can hear them without adding or subtracting, without editing; when you can remember the very worst without cringing, without even an eyeblink of the mind—it's *then* your life will turn. In the meantime you've become too important. You've become too large to misplace.

The mountain peaks curve lightly in a great arc around you and they glisten and sparkle in the afternoon sun. They're still draped in thick white wraps, which soften their forms and cause them to appear even larger against the blue sky. Bits of dark rock and ridge are beginning to show through as the snows dissolve in the spring melt. Faint outlines of cirques push up through the cold white blankets.

There are seven mountains floating coolly in your midst like chilled mirages. It's easy to gaze at them without expecting anything. They are as light and luminescent as an afternoon dream near an open window. Massive and yet lighter than anything within view save the willowy daffodils.

Clouds are moving in now but they're quite high, and the mountains retain a clarity that swallows those who let it. Only those who know how to let go get swallowed. The rest can only look on, somehow apart, vaguely separate, as if viewing a photograph or peering in a shop window. Their thoughts have assumed precedence over everything else. They've become too important and have forgotten what it is to feel their way through life rather than continuing on automatic pilot. Beneath their loud voices and raucous laughter they seem vaguely disquieted as though afraid to be swallowed up by something that is not of thought. Perhaps they vaguely wish that they too could be swallowed for awhile, and yet at the same time they are afraid to be. They would like to know more about it first. Think about it for awhile. They are afraid they might lose their individuality. And so they wait, unaware of their fear, grasping tightly to the handrail of thought. Always waiting for something new to happen, something conclusive. Waiting for something to *break* the silence they could live in. So they wait for something to relieve the emptiness within and they mostly wait in vain. They don't know that nothing new can ever happen for them until they loosen their grip on the handrail of thought. Until they discover how to listen to each thought as though each were but another of the thousand sounds of the night. Or to watch them innocently as though each were but a floating image on a balmy afternoon in early spring.

The clouds are banding together now in the north. They float above the northern peaks like an armada sailing on the deep blue sea of the sky. A hawk is circling high overhead. The sun shines through the translucent wedge of orange tailfeathers. The fragrance of the hyacinths makes your mouth water. The bumblebee has returned with friends. Their separate drones interweave into one thick buzz as they fly around and through the garden. The hawk shrieks sharply, piercing the bees' steady droning where they intersect. The long pine needles make a brushing sound in the wind. The cowbird is chasing a huge black raven. It's flying right up the raven's tail. The raven glides away lazily, unconcerned.

A humble violet is coming up right now. Pushing up in a half-inch space between two volcanic rocks. The white mountains are immense. It's easy to get swallowed when you gaze at them without expecting anything. Of course, it's not the mountains which swallow you, but rather the clarity which has already swallowed the mountains. *Join them there*. Watch. Listen. Let go of the handrail of thought. Gaze at the snowy peaks or anything else and get swallowed. Not by the object but by the clarity of perception. But first you'll have to hear your thoughts as night sounds, or regard them as things seen on a spring day. It may be hard to understand but not hard to feel. It's that which is most basic to you but now lies fallow and forgotten.

Small cloud caps are forming on the near peaks. The hawk is perching in the top of a pine. The violet is vibrating in the warm breeze. To be swallowed by the mountains or the smallest violet is to let go and become insignificant. To lose significance is to return to clarity. To return to clarity is to effortlessly express the inexpressible.

THE EVENING FOREST

THE COOL, DARK FIR forest was bordered by a lush green meadow and a rushing, roaring mountain stream. One sharp snowy finger of the mountain pointed skyward just visible above the tallest trees. The cold stream poured from a glacier somewhere behind that pinnacle.

The meadow was large and almost flat with islands of grey snags near the center and along two edges. A hundred years ago it had been a swamp; a hundred years before that a watercourse of many small streams. Streams that were just beginning to become clogged with reeds and dead grasses. Today it was a beautiful meadow filled with countless pink shooting stars. Someday it would be a fir forest. But today it was a meadow and its thick grass was a green that can only be seen at high altitudes on a clear day beneath an azure sky. The early evening light washed the meadow and the treetops, the gray snags in an orange glow. The roar of the rushing stream seemed both softened and broadened by that luminescence.

Wolf lichen grew on what once had been the living branches of a Douglas fir. The spiraled skeleton of the dead tree formed a trellis for the fluorescent yellow-green of the lichen. A warbler with bright yellow patches perched on the very top in a thick clump of lichen and began to sing. It blended into the lichen perfectly and combined with the evening light and orange trunk to form one being. Singing lichen. A being with no edges, which included you and the entire meadow. A sweetly singing orange light.

The stream was large enough that it was better crossed in the morning before the midday sun would wake and thaw the sleeping snowfields above. Then the melting snows of the warm afternoon would send forth torrents that coursed wildly down the mountainside. Then the falls just below the ford would literally boom. The booming resounded in the mountain valley, echoing, filling it like water fills a vessel.

Everything within that refreshing vessel of dark green forest was immersed in that steady reverberation. Immersed in a divine roar whose endless layers echoed off transparent walls. It's not the sort of sound you can hear solely with your ears. Even to bathe in it won't be enough because there'll still be someone there to interfere, to interpret. To create details. Bathing won't wash beneath the skin. Won't penetrate the facade.

It has to be felt deeper, below the surface, at the very point where all the senses merge. Merge with them right there like a fleck of foam falling into a stream. Just by listening with your eyes you can fold back on yourself and merge into that primal stream of awareness like a river is swallowed by the immensity of the ocean. Only then will you know what point to live from. Only then will you be sure.

Suddenly, a branch cracked sharply overhead—there was a clear bright pause, an unfilled space within your own mind, and then a dull, muffled thud as it finally dropped nearby into the soft reddish duff of the needled floor. Soft greenish-grey moss clung to its cracked scales of bark. A last shaft of remaining sunlight framed the fallen branch, highlighting the broken silvery bark and pale green moss as it lay on the orange duff. The forest light was changing by the moment as the summer evening advanced toward night. It cut delicate, lacy shadows next to a streamlet and for a timeless moment the forest floor was painted a blood red where it met the thick emerald banks. The sun was a red disk floating over the western peak. The snowy pinnacle above the treetops was encased in soft pink alpenglow. The bird that broke the branch clattered through the forest on drumming wings.

There were no people around and the solitude that filled the valley was not lonely, but a living, breathing thing. Everywhere was life. The spaces between things were life. You could feel it in the solitude that filled the valley and coursed through your veins. Everything fell easily within it. Your past history was dissolved in it on contact. A falcon skirted the edge of the meadow and vanished into the far woods.

It was almost dark on an early summer eve and the forest was never more enchanting than now, at dusk. At dusk the mountain begins to withdraw its force back into itself and become quiescent. If you too become quiescent, so still that you can't think of your name, you can feel this as a palpable fact. Just become so still that your mind won't be bothered to remember the mundane and then you'll feel it, like you can feel the shifting of the winds. Then you'll know when the mountain changes from exhaling to inhaling. That's not so important in itself but the mind that is quiet enough to notice *is*. The mind that is not always caught up in detail is your only treasure. Stop chasing details and become still to feel it. The mind that sees details clearly but is not caught by them is like a vast borderless mirror. That mind does not oppose itself.

The half-light of the forest seemed to reveal the essence while it obscured the parts. Sometimes that's easier. For when the pieces become too important, the essence becomes hazy and seems to withdraw. When the pieces become obscured by the half-light of evening, or better yet, by the light of detachment, the essence becomes clear and shining again. The splinters melt back into the whole. The branches grow back into the tree. Plunge in and swallow what hitherto was merely nibbled, piece by piece. Let both life and death arrive and depart suddenly. It's not a matter of acquiring but rather of *losing*. Losing your hold on all that you've acquired. Just making room so the profound can enter and stretch its legs.

The moon rose over a blunt peak and cast its pale light on the meadow. The thousands upon thousands of shooting stars stood next to each other in the thick marshy grass. Their deep pink had vanished now and turned to pale silver as the last wisps of daylight hung on in fragile shreds.

A large doe led several deer out of the black woods at the darkest edge of the meadow. Their soft, liquid eyes held the last glints of the day. Up the slope the waterfall roared its muted evening roar, and the trickle of a dozen jeweled rivulets each contained a separate pale moon in miniature. The dew began to fall and the night air grew cool and damp.

A last dipper bobbed up and down on a wet rock in the spray of the small rapids. It walked directly into the water and disappeared beneath the surface. When your mind lets go of its beloved details, you too can move beneath the surface of things. The bird, a water ouzel, walks on the stream bottom in the rushing current. It feeds there. You too can feed below the surface, in the depths of life, but first you'll have to dive beneath the facade. Just keep on looking, keep on throwing things away. Don't stir yourself up over details. Sooner or later there'll be a flash of recognition and each moon in the water will call you back when you forget.

THE OLD MAN

THE OLD MAN STOOD ALONE on the shore of the alpine lake, mutely gazing out over the silver-white ripples that had just appeared in the afternoon breeze.

He stood at the edge, beneath a summery blue sky, and seemed as much a part of the lake as the rainbow trout, which swam and jumped about in the cold, clear water. Beautifully twisted whitebark pines and conically symmetric subalpine firs supported him, stood with him near the water that lapped the shore.

The old man's gnarled and weathered appearance vouchsafed him immediate membership in an association of old and venerable uprights; seasoned bark, heavy trunks. None of them mere adornments, but rather integral living components of the entire scene, a harmonious collage, which continually shifted, ever-changing with every cloud and ripple that passed and then passed away, as everything always does eventually—everything.

Now his old scuffed hands held his fishing rod lightly but securely, as pine needles adhere to a branch, and he stood gazing out over the lake as though lost in thought, as though immersed in that aspect of the lake that stands beyond its flat surface, beyond its wetness. To separate him, or his tree companions, or the fish from the lake, is to sketch in arbitrary borders, make splinters, lose the wholeness of your mind in the sketch. *Separate them, and you separate yourself.*

When you separate yourself, everything then seems unsatisfactory, for the lake itself was nestled within the ancient mountain within a range of mountains that pushed and rose from the substrate of the earth itself, border after border. You have to glimpse the borders to move beyond; drop one border, then drop them all.

Though he had looked incongruous and a bit bewildered with all his battered gear, the moment he picked up his old rod he seemed to become a part of the lake, like an osprey or a killdeer. Like the waving branches and the ripples that moved together caught in one rhythm, a rhythm which held much more, too much more to grasp with the intellect. It has to be swallowed whole.

So he stood on the shore as if somehow spawned by the lake itself, his rod over the water, his line suspended vertically, swaying over the ripples, his colorful fly caught momentarily in that same great rhythm. Next to the old man, dwarfing him as a parent dwarfs a small child, stood a thick pine with one long branch hanging out over the water. From the edge of the branch hung a long silken thread, and on the very edge of that thread hung a tiny, wriggling yellow worm, an echo swaying in the rhythm of the breeze. The silken thread turned and glittered and became silvery white like the shimmering ripples, and like the old man's line. As his eyes glittered when he turned full-face to the water. They stood companionably, like a pair of fishermen who had fished together in silence for many long years. There was no longer any need for any words between them.

He'd been a little overwhelmed by all his gear and had been grateful for a hand. He offered coffee later—if you happened to be around. And then you left, moving off through the snowy forest toward a white, sheer cliff that hung beneath a huge rock rim. A second lake, smaller,

clearer and greener, lay farther into the woods, closer in
to the snow-laden wall.

The old man was the only one at the larger lake, and
here the prospect of traveling trailless through the snow
had kept everyone out and you were all alone. The sunlight sparkled and dazzled, twinkling like white-hot fireflies over the brightness of the snow and the ever-changing
rippling, shimmering water. The mind was as still as a
dark velvet night, even though it contained the dazzling
fireflies, and even though it contained the very rhythm
that was woven through the entire scene. It contained
every facet of activity, but it wasn't jarred or disturbed by
any of it.

There is a stillness of the mind that is a small stillness
that's only a splinter; a stifling stillness born of repression
or pretense, and it's quite sterile for it's without the power
to create, without the ability to enrich. Time spent there
is wasted, for the splinter is without the perception to see
the essentially nervous quality inherent within itself, a
stillness that can't perceive the borders of its smallness and
cannot move beyond. It's a stillness born of arbitrary borders sketched by pettiness, and it's relatively cheap. You
can buy it cheaply because you sketch it all out. You can
buy it by controlling your breath, or by hypnosis, by
techniques of all kinds. It will always remain a stillness
small enough to fit inside your head, small enough to get
caught in your teeth, small enough to spit out.

But this stillness isn't the one that you gnaw on bit by
bit, but that which swallows you, smashes the gate of your
teeth and makes you smile in spite of yourself; holds, ca-
resses and refreshes you invariably, even when it hurts.

Behind the second lake was a boulder field with car-
sized boulders that had spilled down from the rim wall, a
river of boulders to climb and cross and sweat over. And
then, the river crossed, there was snow again, deeper,
steeper and becoming cooler as you edged toward the

sheer face of rock. The going was slow now, the footing difficult as you climbed higher. Huge chunks of snow broke away suddenly like explosions as integral supports of ice melted away in the afternoon sun. *Avalanche.* Yet the mind would barely flicker at the sharp cracks because you carried your weight low, in your belly, not up in your throat or chest. And though your mind would barely flicker, that barest flicker coursed through your entire body with the slightest tremor, subtly, like a smile, a smile of balance and of readiness. You raised your eyes to the highest ledge of the wall and moved up as close as you dared. The blue-green lakes were coupled far below, like an imperfectly matched pair of eyes, an odd set of breasts. Above, a thick slab of snow was deeply cracked and hung precariously high up on the cliff wall. It would fall, roaring like thunder, in a moment or an hour, or perhaps tomorrow at the latest, then it would pass, like all things have a way of doing. But for now it was held within a readiness to fall or to hang suspended by an unseen thread; suspended, like all of us.

Standing below you shared an involuntary smile of balance, which moved through you like a delicate, thrilling sensation, like a fine tendril waving across your skin. A surge of readiness that calmly glowed within like the glow of a healthy animal. The natural stillness, the real stillness that won't fit under your hat, is the mother of that readiness, and you can't make that vast stillness happen because you can't think it at all. Technique won't get it for you either, but you can let it swallow you, hold you, dissolve your hardened borders, the arbitrary borders that you've sketched in too completely, too thoroughly. The borders that separate, turn you into a splinter. If you know how to return to that vast stillness, you'll be refreshed, cleansed, invariably. Always check on everything to see if it's just another thing to fit inside your head.

The wind had died down now. It didn't fade out, but it seemed to stop all at once as if a switch had been thrown.

When you returned by way of the smaller lake, its ripples had vanished and fallen back into the stillness, and though the rhythm was still there, the time signature was now somehow ungraspable. *Like everything else.* Ungraspable because of passing on.

A round white cloud seemed to breathe above the lake. A small lush meadow was filled with a thousand cream-colored globeflowers and one brilliant scarlet paintbrush. The entire meadow was enclosed by a softly contoured snowdrift. The sun had cut it away, and it displayed a cross-section of agatelike striations, an impermanent record of many new snows fallen on many old crusts over the long winter.

The old fisherman was still at the shore of the larger lake. He stood in the same spot with his gnarled companions and he gazed out over the stillness, which had seemed to engulf him. Holding his rod easily, he defied splintering, seemed part of an immense unity. With each cast of his line, he threw his past out into the water, left his worries there to sink along the bottom and dissolve. When you got closer, you saw that a strange and beautiful transformation had taken place; he was no longer an old man at all—he had cast his lines into the clarity of the lake and shed years and untold burdens. He had learned to cast the deeply etched lines of his face away for a while, and he no longer looked like a gnarled and weathered pine, but stood upright now, like a nobly symmetrical mountain fir. He was quiet, his bewilderment now forgotten. He handed across a cup of coffee wordlessly; steam rose out of a battered yellow plastic mug. You stood together and gazed out over the quiet lake for several minutes without speaking; the silence held you both. He sighed contentedly and said he was originally from California, but that was long ago.

He said that this was the most beautiful spot in the whole world.

THE STORM

THERE WAS ANOTHER WORLD that lay in the space between the two mountains. Another world with rolling plains and roaring ancestral mountain torrents, scores of flowers which managed to look vividly unworldly in the grey light under the slate-blue sky.

The torrents poured from the glaciers down deep rocky gullies, and the grey air vibrated deeply, growling and slapping as it ground away the ancient time-worn rocks, making them smooth and slick to touch. There was no shelter at all in the great openness of the world between the mountains, and the thunder crashed closer than before. The afternoon that had suddenly turned to dusk became daytime again as chains of lightning split the grey sky into jagged pieces of broken slate.

The world lit up for an instant, as if under a strobe light, and in that instant the flowers looked strangely pale in the brilliance of the white light. The pale brightness remained with you for a moment after, and then abruptly, everything turned even darker than before.

A dense curtain of black rain was falling to the southwest, but overhead the laden clouds still mixed and swirled, darkening, growing heavier and fuller as if imminently pregnant with a mountain storm. A half hour before there was but one cloud in the blue sky, and then came another. More appeared by the minute, and their tops flattened out into the anvils that joined together, signaling the coming of the storm. You headed down quickly to traverse the ancient space, the other world between the mountains, and you knew that the only worse place than that broad plain in the storm was the exposed slope of the mountain that you were now leaving.

The scene had been transformed as if by the stark richness of the surrealist's hand, everything woven together with a vividness that actually coursed through your body, made you feel intensely alive. The air crackled with that vividness.

You climbed down the lower slope, taking care not to crush the alpine heather, which cast its diffuse purple over the dark landscape. It was like walking down a sharply tilted artist's palette, a palette that was grey in itself, but was covered with crimson paintbrush, blue and white lupines and yellow cinquefoils. There was an occasional creamy pasqueflower pushing out next to the last patches of melting snow. They mushroomed out of the borderless grey palette, and their elegant simplicity sent ripples of life through the thick electric grey air. It was late in the year for the pasqueflowers, but in the world between the two mountains, snow was still melting in August.

You were on your way down, picking your steps between pink heather and scree, and the sky was the color of dusk, as thunder crashed sharply and the world became daylit again. The scree was the color of the dark sky.

The roar of low, wide waterfalls became broader, deeper. The waterfalls and the sound of thunder, the white-hot flash of lightning and the grey cotton-wool clouds did not struggle but rather consummated their ancient relationship once again, as they have for countless eons, but always freshly, as if for the first time. Can you love that way? *Freshly?* Washed clean like flowers after the storm?

For this is the primal relationship that was born with

the perceiver, the blue of the sky fading rapidly as if drawn out of a tiny hole, and the roar of the torrents as a background. You only perceive them freshly, like the first time, when you enter that expanse of the other world between the mountains, the world of continual emergence, that rock-bottomed essence of your mind, which is always still but ever-emerging. Always there, as if waiting to be noticed.

If you look superficially, wrinkling the brow and tilting the head, or just standing with your mouth open, gawking, the sounds of the thunder, the passing clouds of phenomena and the flashing white heat of lightning will obscure the pristine clarity of things and you'll be disturbed. It always gets obscured when you don't perceive the ultimate stillness of the great performance, and it's even worse if you perceive the conjugal relationship of time and the timeless to be one of struggle. When you struggle against either one you become split in two. Neither gets in the way of the other, and the jagged flashes of lightning flash for but the briefest instant, and yet a timeless instant which contains all and excludes nothing.

The voice of the wind began to howl now as if funneled down the roaring streambeds. The howl of the wind and the rush of the waterfalls mixed and married and formed a symphony that no amount of thought could undo and separate. Together they formed a totally new sound altogether, and it was the freshness of immediate perception that allowed it to be so.

The air across the plain was the strangest mix of hot and cool, and you could feel the two swirling and combining, pushing and pulling the mountain winds in ever-changing patterns. Your neck and arms were chilled and then warmed capriciously as the wind grew hot and then cold again. It ebbed and flowed, but its voice never stopped. The flowers were ruffled about and began to flutter, almost to vibrate. First you heard it whisper, then you heard it roar, the voice of the wind intermingled in conversation with the rushing glacial waters. A conversation beyond the ken of the mind, only because it is a wordless conversation. Can you love like that? With no words, only the rumbling crash of thunder as counterpoint? The primal relationship is one of perception with no concepts to destroy its purity. The rock-bottom essence full of all things unnamed.

The mountain winds and waters, the pure white glacier and the heart of the mountain sing to you of something greater than your tiny precious thoughts. Of *anyone's* tiny precious thoughts.

The first cold drop of rain smacked on your arm, and the next fell in front of a single deep blood-red paintbrush radiant against the grey palette. It thudded into the grey earth, a dark spot appearing instantly.

The rain began to fall harder, accelerating from the rare drop to a torrential downpour within seconds. Lightning flashed across the small plain. The crash of thunder came suddenly and blotted out every other sound like an incredible explosion of quiet. The drumming of the rain became audible again after a small pause, like the dial tone on a telephone. You were soaked now, and you slowed down. The flowers were incredibly vibrant in the soft greyness. You looked at them as you walked.

And you listened.

COMING HOME

You HAVE TO RETURN TO the stillness often to balance yourself out and to keep from becoming as extreme as the jumpy little symbols that pulse through your mind. Return again and again until you come to see that you are really there all the time anyway. Until you listen to the sound of your own voice as if it were small and far away, and the sound gives you no real pleasure anymore, but the *listening* does, the listening contains all the richness that you used to seek. Return over and over until you watch the movements of your mind and find that your thoughts have lost their cleverness somewhere down the line. They still ring, but ring hollow. You're no longer so easily convinced as before, and the brilliance is now in the watching. The brilliance that you sought has remained hidden behind each movement of your mind, hidden in the twisted branches of the continual seeking.

It was late at night and a huge orange moon stood balanced on the horizon of the high desert. The vastness of the desert was palpable in the night air, like the vast plain of the thoughtless mind. The diffuse orange glow was mixed with aromatic sage and juniper and the flat, blunt scent of the sandy, dry dirt. The topmost leaves of sage were individually definable and glowed slightly yellow under the moon. A bat fluttered by, crossing the orange disklike projection screen as it followed an erratic flight path from insect to insect in its wings-on-backwards flight. There were others around, you could hear their high-pitched squeaks in the windless night.

If you return to the silence often, not a small silence that only fits inside your hat, but a vast silence that is big enough to hold you and the moon and the desert floor, if you return to that silence without relying on tricks of breathing or of slyness, it will come to return for you, often. Come to claim you when you least expect it, strip you of everything but the richness and brilliance of listening and watching, partaking of you, drinking you in like a beverage. Many search out quiet to find the stillness, but that way leads only to the small stillness, the one that fits within your skull. The vast stillness is not affected by any activity at all. The activity constantly emerges from it, the stillness that holds everything from which instantaneous action is possible—that's the place.

The moon inched up from the horizon and its orange faded away like morning alpenglow into a pale white. It had decreased in size, but was still quite large in its fullness. The sagebrush in front of you was dark and profiled, but behind you its leaves shone silver like small coins. The mountains gradually became visible as they became illuminated by the pale moonlight. There were three of them and they stood on the edge of the high desert and their snow was like an echo of the silver moon. The snow which reflected the moonlight, which had reflected the light of the sun. Other suns twinkled over the sky, faraway stars almost lost in the moon's borrowed light. If you're impressed by the cleverness of your own thoughts, they become like the borrowed light—what you seek will remain hidden like the sun at night. If you watch them closely and let them go, there will be no such mistake. There's no need to seek quietude, only let go of the rest of that breath that you never seem to let go of and return again and again until you become convinced.

Listen, and fall into the richness of the listening.

Watch, and enter the brilliance of the watching. Just don't get tied to what you hear and see.

The coyotes began to howl in chorus as the moon moved higher in the desert sky. There is something in their wailing voices that vitalizes and intensifies all the senses, washes away the smallness of perspective, cuts right to the core. You could only smell the sage and juniper now if you breathed very softly so as not to chill your nostrils with cool night air. The long, drawn-out howls ended with a series of staccato yips and then returned to stillness, voices out of the very stillness from which you listened. And when you listened from that stillness, they seemed to know you were there listening in on the other end. Once that rapport is established, at the slightest noise or movement you make the whole pack howls as if in reply. Even if you slur your words when you think, they know, and they chorus their strange song in the night with wild abandon as if there's no tomorrow. And without needing to know why, they are right. It's you and they dissolving into the pale moonlight, echoes of one voice in the vast silence.

The night air grew still cooler and the mountains stood silvery clear and sharp like a still life at midnight across the sage.

THE CHANGELESS FLOW

COUNTLESS SHARDS of volcanic glass glittered like a field of diamonds beneath the twin mountain peaks. Their sparkling was intensified by the white brilliance of numerous acre-long snowfields. The morning sun was hot, burning and melting, giving life where life was flowing, drying and consuming the empty husks where life had flowed on, like an endless river. In the shade was a cool chill, the borders of the glittering and the burning, and it was refreshing there. There's always shade for the one who knows that the movement of the river is an endless flow.

There were cliffs of obsidian near a coursing stream that cleaved the snow, but they were in the shade now, and they didn't sparkle. Cliffs of cool black glass, which looked even darker next to the white purity of the snow and the large western pasqueflowers, which stood partially open in the melting snow like creamy tulips. Many were still closed, and their soft coating of fine hairs caught the light and made them look as if they were encased in globes of frosted glass.

You advanced in upward steps of snowfields and lush meadows adorned with scarlet paintbrush and pink mountain laurel. Each plateau of spring meadow was like entering a different locale on a different world, a linked series of fresh wonderlands, all with their own unique views, adorned with their own original flower arrangements. Each insect, every needle and blade of glass, each glittering chip of obsidian and every particle of mountain air emitted a vital freshness that can only be perceived by a mind that constantly emerges, like a year-round mountain spring. A mind like an endlessly coursing river, never stagnant, always fresh.

Grey jays, infamous camp robbers with their dull grey heads and fearless manners, swooped down within feet. A metallic-blue Steller's jay, larger, but wise enough to avoid the aggressive jays, kept its distance and watched hopefully from a tall alpine fir. There was a constant flow of orange-and-black butterflies, which flew by like the endlessly flowing river. A huge dragonfly clung to the scaly bark of a lodgepole pine.

A mind is only new and fresh when it sees its own emptiness, when it relies on nothing to assist its becoming, when it flows without effort and without stagnation. But people look for meaning and security within a locked room in stagnation. They remove bits of the river and keep them in china bowls behind locked doors. Someday they'll need an accounting done, they'll need to determine the value of what they have stored away. If they learn to look clearly, brightly, without attachment, the door will never close again; then they will always know the worth of things, and of open space, and of the flow. There's another way, a more painful way: Keep filling the room, stuff it with memories and imagination, suffering and anticipation; keep filling it, carefully closing the door each time so you lose nothing. One day the room will become so full that the door will no longer shut anymore. Then the things will come spilling out and the light will stream in. And if you let it, the flow will wash away the importance of all the important little things that have remained in the dark, unmoving behind the locked door. Then you'll also know about the worth of things, and of open space, and of the flow. The flow will have carried the door off its hinges as flotsam.

Vibrant patches of purple heather and gentian gave a purple sheen to the meadow below the dark glass cliffs; even those in the shade were deep and rich in hue. The sun had been transmuted in them, given them life and now glowed in a subtle fashion through them. The obsidian was so hard and brittle and only reflected the brilliance of the sun; but still the chips were carried by the flow, glittering, adorning the endlessly flowing river. A hummingbird alighted for the briefest moment on a twig and then was gone, moving away with incredible speed.

The mind is soft, without rigidity, coursing continually like flowing water. Letting life move and change, holding nothing, coming together, moving apart. Mixing, swirling and vanishing like an ever-becoming collage.

There are those who have said that everything is in a state of change. There are others who have said that nothing changes except in appearance. Swallow the two understandings, digest them and then forget them both. Let the hardness be worn away by the rushing, ever-flowing stream.

Butterfly after butterfly fluttered by as if on the winding thread of an invisible highway. The snow on the mountains melts away, and another summer dissolves into a new fall.

THE MIND
OF READINESS

A SLAB OF SNOW broke off the ledge at the top of the sheer wall of rock. It cracked sharply like nearby thunder, just a shade higher in pitch, and momentarily shattered the orderly sequence of time, which the small, complacent mind manages to stuff continually into neatly labeled boxes. The small boxes, with their neatly labeled contents, are always strung out in a narrow line, always balanced on a brink, but few ever notice—notice that they are teetering on the thin edge of an abyss.

It is a brink very much like the snowy ledge that had just given way, rolling down into a crashing avalanche. The air continued to rumble for a few seconds in a series of diminishing echoes, until it finally released the last edges of the vibration and became still again. The birds became quiet in the aftermath, and the aftermath was like a new beginning, a fresh start.

The stillness was not forced, nor was it inertia; it was the state of readiness itself. It brought with it nothing extra, nothing to get caught on, nothing to mumble about later. It worked impossibly quickly, like the reflection of a mirror. It was clean and simple perception stripped of the labeled boxes in the orderly sequence of time. For one timeless moment, everything listened to the avalanche. Some listened with ears, others with whole bodies, still others with surfaces hard or soft like earth, water or rock.

But the mind of readiness isn't quite like any of these at all. It includes them and yet is somehow different, beyond any categories of size, a quality apart from category. The mind of readiness listens also, but listens more like the sky. Listens, encompassing rather than colliding and then chewing. Instant perception with no deliberation. The entry point, the doorway to a different kind of life; a life of richness that hasn't been whittled down to a meager splinter.

The sky holds it all with a marvelous simplicity, so pure and simple that if the brain perceives just a bit of that, it feels immediately that it is poised on the brink. The mind is roused with a great energy that is really its own basic fabric.

Some small rainbow trout, quick as gnats, splashed in the stream. They swam up and down the clear water, two and three abreast, and they moved and turned as one. Suddenly another slab of snow crashed down the wall into the deep white bowl at the foot of the rim. The snow fell gracefully as if in slow motion and left a track on the packed ice and streamed and spattered all the way down. After a lifetime, it hit the bottom.

The rumbling crash of sound seemed slightly out of sync with the fall, like the sound track of an old movie. The mind didn't push against it, but just encompassed it, like the sky. If you push against it you inhale sharply, and for a while afterward you're caught in a struggle to regain your balance. The sudden shock is too great to resist; it makes a dent. It compresses you smaller and tighter, your shoulders fly up toward your ears, and your face looks startled. Each dent takes its toll, and you become smaller, harder, and older. You lose your aliveness; a small mind in a hard body. Your legs are not ready to move, to jump, to avert danger, to seize the moment. All that powers your legs is suddenly moved up into your neck and shoulders, inflating your lungs and freezing your mind. Small actions born of a small mind, really, no better than a twitch or the nervous drumming of fingers.

The mind of readiness is like the emptiness of the sky. Both the stimulus and response arise and vanish within it. Both encompassed by something that is not a thing at all. You're alive within that and ready, like one who knows about the brink and the uncertainty of a perpetual balancing act.

Ready.

Within that readiness, the sounds are held softly, as are the actions and every thought. But there is no twitching, no splintering. There is no way to do it at all, no method for you. Just rouse your mind, let its own energy flow back to itself, like a return air duct. Live in that readiness; not ready for this, for that, for something to happen, but simply ready—ready even for nothing to happen. And ready to return to the readiness immediately when you find that you've become lost in complacency. Let the readiness inundate everything, including the legendary you and the mountains and streams and the stars. Watch them all arise and pass away.

Just for an instant, a quarter moon materialized in the bright blue sky and then was covered over like a slow, exaggerated wink. If you're ready for something in particular, something defined, you can only twitch. Your sense of life is shrunk and reduced in size to fit your skull.

A snag stood in the water, more of a tall stump standing vertically in the deep green glacial water of the high lake. A wind brushed your face and neck and rippled the water. Concentric circles were formed and radiated one after the other, outward from the hub of silvery wood. If you watched closely, and *freshly*, not as if you were looking at something you had seen before, you saw the thin raised edges of circle after circle radiating through the billion ripples far across the lake. Far, far out, they became subtle, less pronounced, but they continued to grow, larger and larger. Their circumferences seemed to outgrow the very shoreline and encompass you on the high bank. The mind was placid; still, yet ready.

For what?

With a sound like a small engine starting, two teal immediately exploded out of a small blind of willows at the edge of the lake. Their strong wings beat like a quickening drumroll. They accelerated to top speed within a matter of yards and flew directly across the rippling green lake and up and over the forested ridge at the far shore under the white, snowy wall. The sky overhead was a deep blue, of infinite depth, and resisted nothing. There were no clouds at all, just a deeply vital blue space, which was unmarked by the traces of flying birds. It was totally filled with the vitality and the birds singing, small particles of moisture, which were mostly invisible but which occasionally caught and refracted the bright sunlight. A rainbow trout jumped out of the water and landed with a slap. Circular tracks emerged successively from its point of re-entry and plowed through the ripples farther and farther out until they finally touched the concentric circles radiating from the snag. They met, colliding with a negligible shock, and then passed right through each other. There was form and energy, but minimal obstruction.

The mind of readiness is something like that; it's relaxed and still, yet alert and potent, like a motionless cat ready to pounce or lunge in any direction, ready to make a pertinent response instead of a previously tape-recorded reaction. A mind like that is flexible, encompassing. A stiff mind is but a hardened core seething with tapes of the past. The hardened center point is a magnet for difficulty, for dirt. A magnet for attracting troubles. All problems dissolve within the mind of readiness, fade and vanish in the vitality. It's ready because it harbors within it no wish to escape, so it encompasses—encompasses and dissolves, with no one to own the difficulty, with no one to escape.

Try to imagine a tiger with a surname; no, there's just readiness, alive and alert, still and yet flowing.

Another trout jumped and smacked down into a dazzling glitter of sunny ripples, which were superimposed on a distorted reflection of rocks and glaciers, snow hanging on a rippling, sheer wall. The glitter looked like hot white sparks flying, or as if there were a blizzard falling upside down. A bullfrog that sounded like a big ratchet croaked hoarsely from a small inlet under a big whitebark pine. Thin raised concentric circles encroached on his tiny cove. They washed ashore with a gentle lapping sound. Several kinds of birds were calling sweetly. A purple finch was visible on a branch of greyish deadwood. A nutcracker seemed intent on shouting them all down. It swooped into the vicinity and the rest fell silent, their tiny melodies stopping abruptly. The bullfrog seemed not to notice or care, but croaked on in his small cove. There was a short lull and then the solitary sound of a hidden bird that sounded like the squeal of a braking train.

The wind made a sudden brushing sound, and the pine boughs and all the sounds emerged from a readiness that was willing to let them arise and depart with no grasping. Animals are all held within that mind of readiness. They know that, and they rely on it, trust in it, live with it. All the dramas of their survival and the play of the clouds and the stars are enacted there. Shoulders stay down, you move quickly, easily, with strong, vital exhalations. The body is strong and limber, the legs are ready to move instead of twitch or stand frozen; you're ready, but not for anything in particular. It's a liberating readiness because pettiness cannot take root in it. You're even ready to re-enter that readiness if you should forget about it, ready to remember again, and ready to encompass what has suddenly caught you and to let it dissolve.

Another piece of the ledge crashed down and fell within the keen alertness of your mind. It rumbled on for a long moment and then became still, sending a pleasurable growl through your whole body. Your legs are relaxed and yet you're ready to spring like a cat. The mind isn't forced into readiness, but is encompassed by it, as if held by the intense blue of the vast open sky.

WALLS

THERE'S A VASTNESS to the mind that is always there when you remember to look. It's not some theoretical emptiness but rather an unencumbered swell whose ripples expand endlessly on. It is neither exclusively inner nor outer, but both at once. The ripples move through the skin line continually, endlessly, and that line becomes an arbitrary border, and you feel the unencumbered swell, you feel the vastness—if and when you remember to look. You can smile then at the thought of the skin line, the unencumbered swell of the vastness moves easily through the skin line as the tides penetrate the three-mile limit. Then there is room to stretch and roam, and the wordless elation of the wild animal just released from captivity. The long sweet exhalation that comes only with freedom, when walls crack and crumble away. All have known it, but for most it remains but an elusive feeling that lies just the other side of the gently swaying reed curtain of memory.

A canyon high up under the imposing face of rock, a canyon both enclosing and unencumbered, a niche hidden away from all but those who journey there. Spectacular shows of a million wildflowers and lush meadows protected by high ridges of conifers. Here you had journeyed into the mountain rather than on it, and you were enclosed, but enclosed by beauty. Enclosed by a vastness that made a plaything of your skin line with its sham borders.

The intense blue of the sky enclosed like an endlessly deep canopy that felt somehow closer than your scalp, seemed to have found its way into the thin space between your throat and the clear sheet of mountain water that you swallowed. It was that rarest of wildflower meadows enclosed in a great hidden room, whose sparkling gems in dozens of varieties seemed to cover every square inch of the lush green canvas, an intensity that short-circuited the wires of memory and released the mind into a vastness beyond the canyon walls.

It was a scene beyond description, with a depth no camera could possibly encompass and capture on flat sheets of film. It was a dense jungle of purple and white lupines, paintbrush of every shade of pink, scarlet, and orange, countless symmetrically creamy cat's-ears. You were stunned and still enough to feel the brain's role in the exchange of color. You and the million flowers seemed but parts of an organic rainbow springing from the ground beneath the layer of grass. Each blossom, every petal, your own feet and hands outlined by the rich green of the grass and brilliant blue of the afternoon sky. There were countless butterflies and bees fluttering and buzzing throughout the flowers. One of the butterflies was yellow and black and blue like the deep blue of the sky above. Hummingbirds moved from paintbrush to paintbrush, attracted only to the deepest reds. The deer merely looked up at you and then resumed eating, all wariness gone as if dissolved by their long stay in this heaven. The big grey jays were fearless as ever, but not so aggressive as usual, as if tempered by the magic of the hidden land. Nowhere was there any fear, as if it had all evaporated in the openness of the unencumbered feeling that was prevalent everywhere. Deep-hued evening grosbeaks, strikingly adorned in amber, black, and white, flew from branch to branch unconcernedly. A falcon glided the length of a long meadow, hunting only yards above the thick waves of wildflowers.

If you allow yourself to get taken up by the vastness, the way one takes up a thread or the strain of a song, you'll come to see the arbitrary border of the skin line. If you let the unencumbered swell move easily past that line often enough, like the tides through the three-mile limit, then that vastness will come to call on you more and more often, until you can never quite forget about it. Then the beauty will enclose you, far after the last of the flowers have faded.

In the evening you saw the big cat move through the forest silently on padded feet. Tail switching, it turned back to look at you. It moved quietly without even the sound of a breath, then bounded, landing with one soft thud, and then was gone.

It roamed the enclosure of the forest, and yet was free and unencumbered, as if always roaming, ranging in the vastness, far beyond the high canyon walls.

BEHIND THE BEYOND

IT WAS HIGH ON THE SHOULDER of the mountain, within a beautiful mixed stand of conifers that delineated the entire scene, for they stood at the farthest edge of sight in every direction. They stood like sentries surrounded by a vast openness, an emptiness that acted upon all that it enclosed. Overhead, the openness was omnipresent and fell and purified the mind, cleansed it of the world far below. The lake had just opened up, and it lay beneath the sky like a new mirror whose shroud had been raised by a hand that was felt but not seen. Ahead, in a great arm that curved about the lake, loomed a huge wall of ice and snow and rock. It stood as a massive barrier of contrast beneath a varied sky of thick white clouds and dark stormy ones, which were splashed here and there with an otherworldly shade of blue. The wind blew straight out of an earlier season, a wind of winter. There was still snow almost everywhere. The huge precipice ahead changed capriciously with the varying sky, its snow becoming soft and indistinct and then sharp and ivory white, like a vision through a camera lens that has suddenly lost and then found its proper focus; yet even the sharpness was in some way held within a gentle softness.

A few tree sentries stood precariously on that huge wall and were dwarfed by it. They changed from flat black to forest green, as the gray and white clouds alternated with the clarity of the deep blue, the dark predominating and then the bright. Everything alternated like that. The openness was everywhere, even between the needles of the trees and in the spaces under the rocks and deadfalls. The needles, the trees and the rocks, everything, was painted clearly on a canvas of emptiness, and the wind roared down the walls, chilling, yet soft and firm like a blow from the palm of a hand rather than the knifelike edge.

The wind became cooler, the sky greyer. Everything was held within a tangible softness, a gentle play of light, even the sharp clarity of ivory white, forest green and otherworldly blue, which still appeared and disappeared, arriving and departing with a mute vibration. A vibration too low to register in the ear. Several killdeer appeared out of nowhere, skimming the lake only a hand's breadth off the waters; they turned sharply, then crisscrossed, then turned again. Another dropped out of the air to the shore of the mirror and walked stiff-legged for two long moments before taking off again; their calls intensely rung out of the emptiness and then instantly dissolved. The boiling cold creek poured endlessly into the lake, roaring along at a lower pitch, an undertone, into which all sounds were led and drawn into harmony. As suddenly as they appeared the fleet water birds were gone, their calls retracted instantly into the emptiness, like notes into their intervals. Living notes sounded on the interval of the roaring wind and the rushing water. When it was time to pass they passed on, leaving only the underlying silence to echo off the icy wall and radiate across the lake.

The wind shifted suddenly, and the blue patches above had all but disappeared. The great mirror of the lake, reflecting the wind and the sky, changed too, its previously glasslike surface broken up into billions of shards of silvery scales moving together like the pliant skin of a huge undulating fish. The great fish swam on and on without destination, through an ocean of sky that had somehow fallen to earth. A soft *click*, and then another, almost imperceptible, and yet somehow fully as loud as the sharp crack and rumble of the shifting ice high up on the wall. Snow began to fall into the bowl of ice and water and trees. Each flake fell directly, without pause, to its place of destiny. *Click!* Each flake fell with a distinct sound that was painted on a white canvas of silence, a silence that was not a mere blankness, but that softly held and assimilated the roar of the descending wind over the wall and the lower growl of the surging creek, which poured over polished round boulders into the silvery lake.

Learn to hold everything softly, like the silence—the way an infant holds onto a finger. Learn to hold so softly that you're not quite sure what is within your grasp. When you can hold everything this way—things, feelings and people—so softly that you forget their names, that you even forget what those things are, then the silence that is the canvas, and the interval on which all things are painted and composed, will hold *you* softly, embrace *you*, permeate you until your very limbs become indistinct from all the other paintings and compositions.

A tall trunk of a dead pine tree creaked, moaning in the rising wind, yet another note in a composition without beginning, sounded on the silence. You hold things softly and are in turn held softly by the basis of every scene you envision.

The sky became softer, greyer, thicker, and so did the wall and the lake and the trees. The sound of the primeval stream was muffled and blended in the wind. There was no harshness anywhere, for there was no harshness in the mind. The snow began to fall harder. The clicks changed into a gentle *whirr* now, and the great undulating fish and the massive arm of rock and ice became softer, completely bathed in a white haze of falling snow.

FOOTSTEPS

THE AFTERNOON WAS CLOUDY-BRIGHT and the air was heavy in the way that only afternoon air ever is. It smelled at once both clean and dusty; both pungent on the flat of your tongue from juniper and sagebrush yet sweet with the ponderosa bark, which smelled like vanilla and looked like burnt cinnamon. The clouds lent a glare to the day that made you squint as you moved across the rocks.

An ancient gorge, deep and narrow, twisted like a writhing serpent. You couldn't tell its head nor tail, but one end twisted far away toward the snowy mountains, toward a far sound of distant thunder, which rumbled down the gorge moving the heavy afternoon air and accentuating the wildness and the desolate beauty of the place.

It was a scene unmarked with time. There was no trace of human beings or of the inevitable debris that marks their passing. A quail called hauntingly, insistently, from beneath a large bitterbrush laden with yellow blossoms and alive with small caterpillars. Wild currants bloomed here with blossoms like coral trumpets. The trumpets quivered lightly in the wind, and the shrubs seemed to blur into the softness of the day.

The thunder grew louder, the sky darker, and the sun became a bright silver disk overhead. The wind made a threshing sound as it passed over the desert floor through sagebrush and evergreens. A tumbleweed was snagged momentarily on some rocks. It strained forward in uneven surges, projected from out of the advancing darkness of the storm. The branches of the tall pines sighed in the wind as their needles whispered, and the leaves of the manzanita rustled in reply. A dry branch below looked like a marten, twisting and moving on a deadfall. It had whiskers of fluorescent-green wolf lichen. Its front paws lunged for an invisible squirrel.

To enter the gorge was to become lost in a timeless desert sea. All traces of your past were battered on the rough rocks, drowned and washed away in the rumbling, coursing air. It was an ancient lava flow, with high snaking walls clearly marking the course of the burning river. At the end of the gorge, which was actually its very beginning, its source, stood a huge volcano, one of several. Its top had blown off, and the ice ages had come and completed the task, cutting it with glaciers and leaving some. It was mostly covered now by snow and ice and looked like a white, jagged crown. It stood serenely aloof over the parched desert like a monarch with amnesia, its nobility unconsciously displayed. From its glaciers flowed clear streams of icy water, which carved life-giving arteries in the dry earth. But this gorge was carved by other streams—streams of boiling lava that flowed from deep within the world below.

Suddenly a pheasant exploded out of the thick brush at the top of the far ridge. Its wingbeats drummed away and faded into the wind. Soft green pines with cinnamon bark, centuries old, stood scattered near the edge. A strange noise emerged from the midst of the long needles into the deepening of the afternoon. The quail still called plaintively as if insisting on something. The wind surged through the gorge in waves, becoming stronger and then quieter in cycles. Every blossom, needle and leaf responded instantly to the rhythm of the breeze. The tumbleweed, still snagged, dropped down the rock into its periodic rest as if preparing for another push. Purple pentstemons with iridescent tubular blossoms grew out of the rock, which was itself covered with a collage of lichens, blood red, orange, bright yellow. Black and grey too, counterpointing the desert mosses, some of which were still green. All of them looked dry, and most felt like the rock itself, but all were alive. You could sense that they were alive in the pulsing wind under the silver light of the veiled sun. They were the advance guard who would prepare the soil of the hard lava, acidify it, break it down. Till the rock, become the soil for the wildflowers and the currants. And then, the ground prepared, a cone would fall from the pines, a berry from the junipers, and roots someday would grab and split huge walls, cleaving them to the small battered pieces that were scattered everywhere below. And the desert would become a forest and the gorge a gully as the rock became soil. It was slow work; some of the lichen took more than a hundred years to cover half an inch. You could see it all happening right now. *It only happens right now*. The tumbleweed, borne on a sudden gust of wind, broke free and floated up slowly, revolving overhead, momentarily eclipsing the soft silver disk of the sun.

There was no defined path down to the floor of the gorge: Like what we call a "life," the path sprang into being only at the very moment you placed your foot down. If you stopped moving, it ceased to materialize for you. Like what we call a "life." Meanwhile, the path behind dropped off as you left it—faded away and dissolved as you moved. It was dry and it crumbled away behind you as you walked. There was no going back. You were left stranded on a small island of the present. *Left where you belong*. The island had no shores, for it stretched omnipresently everywhere yet it was also quite small, for it was just the space beneath your feet. It left you standing on an endless universe the size of a flagstone. It was like that because you were alive in the present. The path of living really is a path with nothing, absolutely nothing, ahead or behind. Let the past fade from your back and move freely without constraint. The world of the present, the only place on which to stand, is prior to even the past. Let the footprints behind you dissolve and let the path materialize for you as you tread. Don't be afraid of that small island with no shores, for it stretches far beyond the ranges of thought, unfathomably wide and deep. It will always be large enough to contain the entire unsplintered present. It will always contain all of the mystery itself.

A pair of warblers sang a duet as the wind picked up, howling now, swallowing up the drumming of the quail as it disappeared over the ridge. The pathless path down the gorge, the living out of a "life," continued to dissolve behind as it materialized. The thunder drew closer, deeper, like a growling deep in your own chest and throat. Drops of cold rain began to fall on the dry floor of the gorge. They seemed to fall right through you. Pentstemons shimmered in the breeze. They felt like fine hairs quivering on your arm. The pines and sagebrush sighed and whispered and rustled within as your own thoughts. A red-shafted flicker shot by, white under the tail, day-glow orange beneath the wings. A flash of lightning suddenly emerged from beneath its orange feathers. Your footprints faded away in the storm. Your past dissolved behind you, and you had become the essence of everything around you.

THE LAKESHORE

THERE IS A TYPE OF PERSON who is at home with impermanence, who wears the clothes of impermanence well,
dressing and undressing easily, changing costumes without attachment as circumstances change. One who moves
naturally with the endless flow of events, never stagnating
yet inwardly unmoved by the multitude of changes continually occurring within and without. A person like this
holds no rigid views, and so is able to walk on ahead of the
past rather than merely plodding along behind it. Hence
they are able to view things freshly, unhindered by the
past. Though they are aware of what has gone before,
they are not held in its sway. Their minds are big and
broad, uncramped, vast as space. Perceptions, and
thoughts that arise from those perceptions, pass through
the vastness like meteorites, but they are like mere dots
arising and disappearing within an endlessly open landscape. Everything arises and then vanishes; everything
passes on through the spacious mind that's at home with
impermanence.

Someone like that doesn't dwell in the shadowland,
doesn't live within the ephemeral shadows cast by memory and imagination. The world of the past and future.
They are alive here and now in the present moment. They
literally *are* the present. Their lives unfold and flow with
each passing moment.

They have ceased suffering the pangs of the past and the future. Though they have pain, it is always the pain of the present. It is only the pain that they know to be impermanent like everything else, rather than the mind-pain that results from resisting impermanence, futilely swimming backward against the flow of change. They no longer suffer the pain that results from not being at home with change, the pain that is inherent in seeing the little self as changeless and permanent. Though it may truly ache, it hurts only in the moment. Since there is no storage of old pains as memory, and no projection of them into the future as imagination, that person remains unmarked, virginal, as the years seemingly flow by.

An unfolding mystery continually emerges: a perpetually fresh and clear mountain stream flowing by a serene observer sitting on the bank; a perpetually clear mountain stream flowing on past itself, watching itself flow by. A motionless observer watching itself flow down the stream; an observer confronting its own essence wherever it turns, yet just taking everything just as it is and creating no problems where none exist. A mystery continually emerging like a spring.

The eagle was very large. It glided and banked over the mirrorlike surface of the placid lake. Its movement was the very embodiment of grace itself. It banked and dove steeply in traceless trajectories that were somehow miraculously devoid of angles, every increment of its soaring flight absorbed into the radii of huge curves. It flew past effortlessly, hardly moving its great wings in the still, cool morning air. Mist was still rising from the lake here and there, looking like wisps of smoke from small cook fires. Brand new purple lupines bloomed around the lakeshore. They thrived in the barren, sandy soil.

It was a bald eagle and as majestic in its presence as the lofty snow-white mountains that formed the backdrop for the placid lake. They appeared cool and light like substantial mirages, as if aloof from the grime of the world, chastely clothed in the recent snows of early spring. The eagle's stark white head echoed the snowy mountaintops ahead and the very whites of the clouds drifting above.

And there were mountains in the water too; cool and fresh and upside down, perfectly reflected in the glassy surface of the steaming lake. The lazily rising mists looked somehow otherworldly and cast a dreamlike veil over the scene. One thick wisp of steam seemed to emerge from the very top of the mountainous reflections, a white volcano ready to erupt into the placid lake. The eagle flew around and through the shreds of steam while its reflection flew around and through the snow-white mountains in the lake. Its white hood would disappear for moments at a time as its mirror image soared across the surface of the reflected snows. It seemed to be flying too near the volcano, oblivious to any danger. There had just been another storm in the mountains; their lupines were still buried under several feet of snow.

A school of a thousand minnows flashed red, then glinted silver, as they turned as one in the shallows. A lone killdeer dropped suddenly out of nowhere, then shot off over the water in a long bounding arc like a checkmark fallen over on its side. The minnows scattered, agitating the surface, and the sky in the water turned quickly to a murky grey. The mountains in the lake were shattered into small white bits that floated choppily on the surface. The mountains standing in the backdrop, however, remained unmoved. They still stood majestically intact, aloof, mirage-like.

A whole flock of killdeer followed the first ones, arriving abruptly and taking over a thin peninsula of deserted sandbar. Their long, high-pitched calls pierced the scene and cut sharply through the still morning air. Their calls lost their shrillness against the shattered bits of broken mountains in the lake. Deprived of contrast, they blended there easily. They alighted momentarily on the sandbar and then exploded into flight together. Their underwings were crisply marked and flashed like Navaho blankets airing against the increasingly hazy morning sky.

The mountains became a softer white against the thick cumulus clouds moving above and between them. The killdeer too, viewed from a distance, now appeared softly shaded, almost pastel, in the cloudy brightness of the morning sun. A gentle rustling sound emerged from beneath the lush alders near the shore. The minnows became lost to the eye in the soft grey water. The wisps of steam were vanishing, the volcano became dormant. Softly flowing linked phenomena passed, a continual nexus arising and vanishing, perfectly interwoven with no ragged edges showing anywhere. *Nothing is really ever out of place if you don't hold onto it when it wants to depart.* Just kiss it all hello but don't embrace it, just wave good-bye but don't clasp hands. Then the mind becomes still and thoughts give way to the stream of perceptions flowing serenely by. Flowing serenely by each other. *Where will you stand to watch?* Perceptions like countless facets of a softly glowing gem, facets that never obstruct one another.

But the eagle did not share visually in the softness. Everything about it looked sharp and clear and well defined as it skimmed over the water. Like the mountains sometimes appear to do, it gave the illusion of growing larger as it receded farther away toward the far shore. It still looked crisply white and brown as it flew between the soft grey of clouds and water. It supplied its own contrast born of sheer presence in spite of the haziness of the sky.

The flock of killdeer, picking in the sand of the shore, studiously ignored it as it circled near them and then flew off across the far shore and out of sight. One moment the eagle had reigned majestically over the lake, silently gliding above the glasslike surface; the next moment it was gone, vanishing between the tall pines at the edge of the lake. Its powerful presence broke apart and dissolved instantly as it disappeared from view. One very pale blue patch of sky marked its point of departure.

The lake reflected it all clearly like a mirror. There was no wind to ruffle the tranquil glasslike surface. Individual spring-green willow leaves were reflected clearly near the water's edge. When the surface becomes ruffled it cannot affect the hidden depths but still there is distortion, and the images of pure, cool mountains are broken into shattered white fragments. The mind seems to become murky and ceases to reflect faithfully when it holds onto even one of the myriad things that are forever passing peacefully through. Even the difficulties and the pains come and go peacefully if you let them. If you don't push or pull on things. If you cease swimming backward into the past. Don't dwell in the distorting ripples of memory and imagination, but always return to the still point of the present. Let things be just the way they are. Let the eagles and the clouds arise and depart when they will. The lake had reflected it all clearly and then let it go easily, instantly, as it all departed.

Now a flock of ducks was reflected on the mirror of the lake. They approached from the south and flew low over the surface before braking. Their wings beat a powerful drumlike rhythm totally unlike the eagle's or the killdeer's. Unlike too, the insistent rustling sound beneath the alders. They dropped and settled down, merging into their own images in the mirror. Reflected and reflection eased together and became one. Each left a long, clear landing trail in the water. Ripples danced and then faded as the ducks swam peacefully in the lake, heads randomly bobbing beneath the surface. The water is buoyant but does not oppose. Where there is no opposition things happen easily. Things follow each other, move through and past each other harmoniously. Watch it all intently but let it all be, like watching a dream.

A quail called out plaintively from the dense under-brush beneath the alders. The rustling sounded again, softer than before. The ducks exploded into flight, each pair of wings tracing a letter X from behind. They still flew low over the water. When they fly low like that it usually rains. The clouds were becoming greyer and thicker above the lake. A west wind came up and busied the surface of the water. The mountains seemed to chill suddenly and become colder, whiter, like the stark white of the eagle's head. The mountains in the water frag-mented and became totally indistinct in the breeze. Yet the mirror of the lake still reflected perfectly, only now it ceased to portray the sharp clarity of objects and began to show clearly the distortion caused by the wind. Just as the clarity of your mind will perfectly reveal the distortion caused by the winds of thought. Reveal easily the waves and ripples borne on the breeze of attachment to what has been.

Just come to see that everything is passing on. That nothing in your mind remains the same for even the span of a breath. If you see like this for even a moment, then for that moment you are free. Don't let a day go by with-out resting in a tranquil watchfulness, witnessing every-thing like an alert tree. Like an unruffled lake. Or like a ruffled lake aware from its depths of its distorted surface. Don't make an eagle something better to see than a moun-tain—or a mistake. Lubricate the mind with the oil of detachment. Lubricate it so nothing sticks whose time has come to leave. Let it all roll by like a film. Let it vanish like a dream upon waking. Don't stop anything from leaving. *Even the mirror*. Just watch from no particular vantage point. Participate when you must but gracefully, alertly, like the eagle soaring on the breeze over the tranquilly watching lake.

The quail scurried out from the underbrush beneath the alders scratching at the earth. Moments later another shyly looked out but made no move to emerge. The faint rustling sound continued, broken by one melancholy sounding call. A red-shafted flicker traced a scarlet line against the grey sky and then clung to the side of a tall thick pine. The air felt suddenly heavy. A nearby water-fall roared as if in a dream. It had been there the entire time. It hadn't stopped for a moment. *You'd only been standing on the lakeshore for several minutes.* Everything moved easily past. Just sitting on the bank of a stream watching yourself flow by.

THE EDGE

IF YOU LET YOURSELF get caught up in a search it will always elude you. But that doesn't mean you shouldn't watch—you *have* to watch. And listen too. Closely, continually, intently. You'll have to learn to read life between the lines, dissolving barriers, growing simpler rather than accumulating more. You won't be so entranced with your own knowledge anymore and confusion will drop away bit by scattered bit. When you run out of confusion, things will become clear. Be careful in your use of concepts; like a sword, it's dangerous to hold the cutting edge. Cease adding mindlessly to your precious stockpile. Let it all blow in the wind, riding the currents like ashes and thistledown, and from then on you'll never lose that deep sense of belonging. A belonging that relies on nothing, nothing at all.

You'd fallen into a scene of unsurpassed beauty. The mind had melted into the scene and become homogeneous with it. The mind became the belonging itself and the belonging permeated the scene as naturally as the vibrant greens of the firs permeated the early spring meadow.

The unsurpassedness only arises when the mind becomes totally still. Still, yet incomparably alert and alive, melted into the beginning and into the scene itself. Borders disintegrate when the mind no longer accepts the hardened boundaries of thought as final. When the mind becomes still it quickly forgets its acquired smallness, which permeates and encompasses everything. Everything all at once, even the belonging.

Just ahead towered the sheer walls of an ancient volcano, which seemed to have fallen into itself. It was a stunningly rugged mountain, a bizarre distortion out of a Chinese landscape, fluted with organ pipes and rocky towers. Small forests of ancient firs clung to random outcroppings of rock on the sheer north face. It was an extinct volcano now or maybe just sleeping for awhile. A great molten core of lava, the plug, had settled back into the center as it cooled and had become the face of the mountain itself. The shadowed face had newly fallen snow on top of the old, and there were complex markings like giant undecipherable petroglyphs where boulders had rolled wildly down, crisscrossing the walls of snow.

The face was a complex mass of snowy medieval towers and needlelike pinnacles. The topmost edge of summits resembled the spine of a colossal stegosaurus with rows of vertical armored plates. It was mostly rust red, dripping everywhere with fresh white snow. Every crevice and hollow was caulked, each ancient cirque was filled with snow like bowls of thick white cream. The whole fantastic structure shot up vertically and abruptly from the meadow floor like an immense headboard. At its base was an intricate system of interconnected meadows and small rushing mountain streams, tiny glacial lakes separated by elegant stands of firs. The meadows were mostly covered with snow, which surrounded random islands, green oases of spring. It was like something out of a rare dream, so lovely it could have made your heart ache if you could not enter into it. But with a mind that's still and mixed with its surroundings, there was no ache at all, just a serene sense of belonging.

There were fresh coyote tracks in the snow. A woodpecker sounded through the meadow, hammering on a bare, sun-bleached snag. It was not feeding but rapping slower and more deliberately. It was announcing its presence, staking out its territory.

A dipper contemplated the singing water as it bobbed up and down in the shallows. It suddenly ran on in and disappeared below the surface. Butterflies crossed over the stream at one spot as if across an invisible bridge. The bulk of the mountain filled the foreground and stood with its huge castlelike walls and moat covered with snow and blotting out a large piece of sky. The armored dinosaur plates looked crisp and sharp against the cloudless blue expanse. The sun was hot overhead even though there was cool white snow almost everywhere. The air was summer while the ground was still in winter. Nearby was an alpine lake, thickly frozen at one end with striated mounds of drifting snow piled on top. The ice grew gradually thinner as it approached the near bank until it became a blue crescent of thin cellophane sparkling in the bright snow light.

A scene from a dream. A white wonderland with a hint of spring that knelt and paid homage to the stark monolith whose melting snows allowed its lushness. The islands of spring were opening like eyes in the meadow. In them hellebore was still pointed tightly and shot up like reddish-green missiles. Thick patches of both pink and lavender phlox bloomed in lovely heaps next to the crusty snow.

Something darted by low and fast at the near edge of an adjoining meadow. Something that was only there for a brief instant and then vanished into the trees. A squirrel scolded the apparition from the trunk of a fir. A jay darted out of the brush hurriedly.

The mountain presided over the landscape so vividly that it seemed to be an illusion of rock and snow conjured up to fill a void. A hologram to fill a bare place in the universe. A real illusion, one you could fall from. A void was just somewhere your thoughts couldn't reach at all, some place left uncreated and unhandled by knowledge. Some place *here*.

The peak stood against the sky like an enormous cutout behind which lay the unknown. An unknown that did not lie merely ahead, but also *behind* the eyes of the one who listened and watched. When you become caught by what you see and hear, when you become lost in your thoughts, you diminish the world. Then the far ridge of the mountain and the eyes of the watcher mark the circumference of a sphere of the mundane. Both then lie on an orbit of beginning and ending, a mean circle of tired knowledge. A circle much smaller than most would dare to hope.

Yet beyond your thoughts, untouched by history, is a beyond that lies outside the orbit. You have to relax into it. And the periphery of that beyond is right here, right now, and it passes behind your eyes, through your core, directly through your heart. It turns continually so that the unknown beyond and the unknown within constantly exchange places and become just two aspects of one limitless something. Intuit it, but don't chase it—let it come to *you*. If you pass beyond that circle without budging an inch, you'll enter a vast clarity that excludes nothing. *Not even illusion*. But first you have to see the borders of your smallish world, the circumference of the sphere, in order to pass beyond. See clearly the boundaries of the island, and you will simultaneously see the immense sea. To pass beyond you have to see the edges of your mundane world of thoughts.

A dozen different birds sang more than a dozen different songs from a hundred places in the snowy meadow. The ice on the alpine lake had grown thinner and thinner in the midday sun but was still barely frozen at the closest sunny edge. Brown ants carried a black horsefly through a thick jungle of new grass, and then the coyote appeared, trotting across a small opening. Lean and scraggly, it must have had a long hungry winter. Intelligence danced in its eyes. It was a survivor, scraggly or not. A warbler sang in a tree above you and sang sweetly. Each note rang clear and bright. Everything was held in a serene belonging.

When things become achingly lovely, it means you've fallen back within the old circle, imprisoned within the small sphere of history. It's the sense of separation that aches. When you let go of the contents of the circle everything feels serene. Then even the circumference dissolves and illusions become the truth. The art of life is to know the borders of the mundane sphere, to keep the narrowness from taking over your life.

One large purple trillium was illuminated by a yellow sunbeam that streamed through the thick branches of the tall firs. Nothing could add to its innocent beauty, to its belonging. But if you get caught up in any search at all, it will always elude you, looking for unsurpassed beauty with a chattering mind.

CIRCLES

IT WAS VERY WINDY at the top of the rocks. It wasn't a wind that blew from any certain direction, but rather a swirling wind, a spiraling wind that moved in and out through the shrubby vegetation below, following thread-like paths through countless appendages and spiraling up the tall pines whose tops were now at eye level. They were soft and green and long needled. And the needles quivered as the branches swung around and around in tight circles. The swaying of the tall trunks was not actually on a line but in another circle; the treetops inscribing a faint circumference around the base of the trunk far below. The very bottom of the trees appeared to be motionless, countless center points for countless circles, but they vibrated softly and you could feel the hum of the vibration from clear up on top of the rocks.

It seemed to be a world of circles. The vortex of a dust devil levitated far below. A neat round sink of precious water lay carved in the rocks several feet down. It was the size of a hand and it glistened in the sun. It held three small suns and a white, snowy moutain, which gleamed on its surface. Ants scurried round to its rocky shores. They looked like skittish deer gamboling at the edge of an alpine lake. There was also some sand around the lake, only the sand was brown lichen, which adorned the rock. There was even a miniature forest, though it had grown slightly out of scale, a forest of green and purple, a pentstemon forest shimmering with iridescent blossoms.

There were mountains ahead and they were ivory white with flat black, sharp against the clear blue of the sky. They looked like great fortresses of snow and ice. They felt closer than any measurement of distance could define. There was no feeling of watching them, they were too close for that. You could feel them though, as if they were not outside you. They felt like a lump in your throat. When you get too close to them, you are right on top of them and you are too close to see them anymore. When you get too close to things your vision suffers. At any rate, you have to know just how much vision to use. Too much, and your eyes become hardened and your mind is there interfering. Too little . . . go ahead and try for too little, then you *might* feel them and you might disintegrate easily and lightly into that feeling. Go with it. A circle with no center and no circumference. Don't try to make anything vanish to try to find that circle. You can't. Let everything be just the way it is for a while. That's the way to get the center and the circumference at one shot.

A red-tailed hawk appeared and turned circles in the swirling wind. It dropped down far below and then spiraled up to eye level, even with the tops of the rocks and trees. The circles had no center at all; there was only a deep powder blue. And they had no periphery either, for that edge faded away behind the big hawk's tail. The very last edge of tail feather became the past, and the past can't be held by anyone or anything. It's only the present moment dissolving away.

The hawk flew in front of a snow-white mountain and its tail became a thick wedge of burnt orange, like the bark of the older pines surrounding the craggy rocks. The wind picked up suddenly and swirled around in strong gusts and rose and descended in invisible spirals. You let yourself be buffeted like the trees and the shrubs, like the tiny lake. If you didn't fight it, the buffeting was refreshment itself. If you didn't fight it, there was no one around to complain. No problems at all then. Just the fullness with no one pushing. No strain. The forest of pentstemons was especially good at bending. The glowing purple flowers became richer and richer in the swirling life of the mountain wind. A billowing white cloud bank dropped to one side of the mountains. Somehow the wind blew the peaks even closer. You got the lump out of your throat and breathed them in and out.

Down below at the base of the pines the snowbrush was in full bloom. It grew in thick clumps around the lava, hugging the base like a thick white ring. The hawk disappeared somewhere in a hanging cloud. The miniature alpine lake rippled and tossed the suns and mountains around effortlessly. The shores of the hand-sized lake were now deserted. The ants had crossed the brown lichen sand and vanished into small cracks in the rock. There were more circles than ever now. The wind blew chokecherry blossoms off one by one and they swirled crazily around, dancing in the lively wind.

OVER THE EDGE

STREAM FOLLOWING again. Another stream on another mountain, climbing higher through the snow to another spring glacier. Again? Of course, "again" is only an appearance, one moment in a flow of moments contained within an endless presence, like the stream that passes you while sitting on the bank, a stream that flows at all points, at all places. Those points are the moments, just movements within your own mind.

The day was sparkling like crystal in the sunshine so that you also sparkled within easily, lightly, with no effort at all. It was one of those mountain days when the sun shone bright and very close, and it was buttery yellow in a sky that was so blue it seemed like the sky of another planet, a planet that you hadn't yet destroyed with familiarity. The deep blue seemed to be alive and to interact with everything, both moving and still. You could almost breathe it in. The rich green evergreens stood vibrantly sharp and clear against the sky, shades of green and blue you can only see on a certain kind of day high in the mountains. On a day when you might as well be on another planet because you aren't destroying everything with your familiarity, cursing everything with your exalted knowledge.

The air was exhilarating in the most subtle way; it was that rarest of spring days, snow almost everywhere, a sharply descending mountain stream with countless cascading waterfalls, a warm sun and a cool refreshing breeze that somehow tasted mild and sweet. It sang in the bent treetops like a wraithlike alto muse; it was at once like bathing in a cool caress that was both a soft sound and a delicate fragrance. You had to inhale slowly, very gently, to smell it. Your mouth watered and there was a slight tang in the back near the root of your tongue.

There was no one at all for miles and miles. It was still early to be up here, so there were no others to hear the rushing, roaring music of the stream and see the spray of cold, clear droplets filling the streambed just below. They caught the sunlight and transformed it instantly into a mist of minute rainbows. Each drop became the agent of a multitude of colors by refraction, yet each retained its own clear purity and essence, unaffected by the multicolored tints, as a projector lens remains unaffected by the contents of the film, as the mind remains unaffected by the contents of its thoughts.

The snow on the bank was similarly unaffected. Just a sounding board and projection screen for the roaring rainbow mist that emerged from the plummeting stream. The stream appeared and disappeared under thick mounds of snow that had just begun to melt. The mounds looked like great white tortoiseshells whose occupants had curiously vanished, taking with them legs and tails. The icy water poured out of the dark holes left vacant.

There were other ridges and behind them flowed other streams, each running in its own carved furrow of emerald and white, each a separate flowing crystal world flowing from the snowmass to its intersection with another flowing world at another fork below. A joining, and then a new world emerges roaring louder and deeper than before, an ever broader world as each fork adds its own touch to the shape and the flow of the stream. And yet the flow is unaffected, continual, inevitable. Like the life that seems shaped by events but is also the life force that is untouched by them.

A warbler with bright yellow markings darted from one nearby pine to another, as if looking for something lost or misplaced; or perhaps for something it never had, but wanted. No time to warble now, just a quick conversational chirp, more like a click, in passing. Dozens of monarch butterflies flew around the stream. The orange on their wings was intensified by the blueness of the sky. They flew determinedly in the fragrant wind and then settled down to perch here and there, wings lining up perfectly with the wind. The waterfall seemed to get louder and move slower as you stood there until you were inundated by its slow-motion roar. It carried each and every thought over the edge. Your thoughts flowed over the edge and were gone in the churning water below. They flowed away continually until they began to lose their meaning, like a word that you repeat over and over again. All the power and movement of the falls vacuumed out the mind, and it became totally still. The falls fell through that stillness unhindered; you only knew that later by a sort of hindsight, and because later you felt totally refreshed.

Perhaps the thoughts are carried far away downstream where they will collect in a pool or on a bank and transform themselves to other things. It doesn't really matter; they're of no use to you anymore. Energy is never really lost anyway. Now is the time to explore the stream, to search for the place where the thoughts arise. The snowmass. It's not the kind of thing you can know with your head, and that very unknowing, that ungraspability, will keep you on the brink where you belong, falling and ready to fall, totally refreshed each moment in the ever-flowing of the stream.

A mountain chickadee flitted around agilely, its black hat looking as if it might blow off in the breeze. It flew higher as if rising by stairsteps, as if it were suddenly drawn up to each new plateau from above. A snag creaked in the wind and the warbler seemed now to have found what it had been looking for. It flew off with a newfound friend upstream toward the snowmass, moving eagerly back toward the source.

JOURNEY ON
MIND MOUNTAIN

THE BEST TECHNIQUE is manifested unconsciously rather than merely displayed. The best skill is one that has been fully absorbed and naturally comes to permeate one's life, as a plant photosynthesizes sunlight and becomes pervaded by its energy throughout. When you cling to technique, it immediately becomes a shackle, just another set of chains to escape. If, however, it is absorbed and used naturally without depending on it, it becomes an enrichment.

If you come to the study of technique with an open mind, without the drive to become, you are already studying beyond the narrow limitations of technique. Through this open study of technique you may come to see your unnecessary complicating of that which is originally simple and straightforward; how you have constructed your world from the fabric of habit and then taken it for granted. And through this deep but open study of technique your course becomes smoothed out; skillfulness in the tasks of daily life removes superfluous jounces and jars and allows the mind to function smoothly, out of stillness.

But there can be no attachment to the technique itself. No attachment to a someone you will become when the skill is acquired. Rather the skill must be absorbed and manifested rather than displayed. Skill in the actions of daily life enriches, and the best technique allows the mind to lighten its load. The best skill is to be simple in one's actions, devoid of graceless wheel-spinning born of opposing thoughts.

It was that clearest of early mornings. Clear and cold through and through. The firs wore their darkest shade of green, each flat, striped needle sharp and distinct against the cloudless blue sky. Inch-high blades of silver hoarfrost grew out of the frozen forest floor, packed tightly together like a rich lawn of finely glazed crystals. The snow, which had been melting away of late, had refrozen last night leaving an armorlike crust of ice. A crust so hard it left virtually no tracks at all.

If you know the early morning sub-alpine forest in early spring, you know how every shadow can fill with crosshatches of ice awaiting the sun. You know too, how your back, still lagging in winter, is bitten by the morning chill even as your face is warmed by the low spring sunshine and how the northernmost side of every tree trunk has grown a thick silver pelt of frost.

The mountains teased; one was visible *here* through the trees, and only *here*. Another was visible only *there*, exactly from that very spot. They came and went, arising and vanishing through the morning as you walked. They stood so clear and white, so fresh in the icy clarity of the morning air, that you were stunned as if by a blow each time they reappeared. Your mind was stunned into a broad silence as still as the frozen morning. They beckoned, drawing you forward, closer and closer over the path of hoarfrost, which broke and almost rang like delicate shards of glass beneath your feet.

A large doe looked up suddenly, startled as you approached her through the trees. Her head shot up as if a spring had been abruptly released. She broke into the first two steps of a run and then changed her mind and stopped. She just stood there, watching you intently. You both stood there watching each other, and then she finally turned suddenly and walked away. The muscles of her hindquarters rippled as she moved off through the dark woods. She didn't look back, but she *listened* back for a sudden movement, for the slightest crack of a twig. One moment she was there, ears pricked, head high, and the next she had vanished into a thicket.

Walking, the mind is naked, bare and fresh like new-fallen snow. Or like bright new crystals of silver frost. Walking, you become effortlessly aware of the forest and the doe; of the white mountains and the blue sky; of the soles of your feet and the hard earth packed beneath them. Effortlessly aware of the whole stream, the causeway of phenomena that passes by serenely. That passes as you walk onward. And then, finally alive to the living fact of direct perception, you come to feel the entirety of the world interpenetrating your thin line of skin.

Most have little awareness of the finer points of walking. The walking that clears the mind of thoughts, the walking in which you knowingly participate. To most, walking is merely something that they learned years ago, unconsciously, and have not refined at all since. Most have not learned since but rather have forgotten the natural way to move. Most don't know how to look directly to watch the product they are turning out day after day. If they can't watch, they can't navigate, and so they accumulate layers of habit year after year on automatic pilot.

There's a peculiar combination of lightness and heaviness necessary to move well. The knees slightly bent and flexible like shock absorbers. The belly heavy while the head is light. Light to steer with, light to see softly with. Light so as not to interfere. The tight neck muscles of a heavy head will oppress you, stifle your life and movement like a ruthless despot. The discomfort will gnaw at you, irritate you insidiously into closed circles of thought. You'll forget you're walking, you'll forget to look. You'll just plod on, vaguely aware that things are somehow not as they should be.

Too many drag their heels. They're always a step behind the arising and vanishing because they don't know how to move lightly, weight forward, ready to leap. Each step is the very beginning, the first increment of an agile leap. Then the mind is tuned just right, when each and every step is the beginning of a leap into infinity. The weight is toward the ball of the foot and the mind is ready to spring lightly in any direction like a cat. Few know how to walk into infinity because they are always walking behind the thick wall of the past. The wall crowds them when they attempt to keep up and pushes them back on their heels. They're stuck behind the barrier of the past because they have ceased looking and learning. Having a body, they know little of its use. The body compressed, the mind easily becomes cramped and loses its spacious quality. It is only technique, but technique blends into skill, which is absorbed and radiated. Skillfulness, when there is no attachment, smooths the jagged edges and makes it easier to watch with pure intent. Easier to watch from the stillness that allows everything to be as it is.

The creek sounded like deeply resonant chimes ringing through the narrow gully. At first, when you were still some distance away, the sound was more like the wind rustling through the trees, but as you drew nearer a lilting music commenced, emanating through layers of the water's ancient roar and ringing bell-like throughout the wooded valley. You walked through the sound as you crossed the icy creek, immersed in it, as though walking through the fine spray of a waterfall.

The silver blades of frost were losing their sharpness and becoming shorter and thicker as they began to melt into the advancing day. A big woodpecker clung to the side of a dying tree near a bend in the rushing creek, his scarlet crown brilliant against the dark green firs. He picked soundlessly at an existing hole. His pale breast under mottled dark wings was a chip off the snow-covered mountains where great ridges and dark boulders punctuated crisp white blankets.

Another doe, smaller than the first, peered out from a tangled clump of young firs, chewing and watching. She backed away reluctantly, still chewing, and faded deeper into the forest, vanishing as you passed. You didn't look back but *listened* back, allowing your hearing to sharpen. A branch cracked sharply and was followed by the bounding thump of twin hooves on the forest floor. The thump resounded throughout you intimately, like your own body's heartbeat. Learn how to listen on the periphery of your hearing, listening both *to* and *from* the realm where seeing and hearing blend into one. Listen intently with the wholeness of your perception rather than with your ears alone. When you listen like that, you don't become caught, the arising and vanishing of the mountains flows on unbroken, and the mind retains its expansiveness. Walk on, flowing forth, listening and watching, letting everything arise and fall away as it will.

A raven squawked importantly high above, circling across the blue sky, hawklike, around and around in the spacious foreground of the four crisp snow-laden mountains. An iridescent sheen moved in wavelike patterns across its jet-black body as it coursed through the rays of morning sunshine. A whiskey jack fearlessly accompanied you down through lanes of cool forest shadows, moving alongside from tree to tree, half hopping, half flying, from one branch to the next. Each new perch the beginning of a leap to the next. Each step an arising and vanishing in the present, unescorted by any shred of the past.

Learn to feel the *feeling* of moving freely. How can you have a broad, spacious mind when the body is small and cramped? A mind of the unfolding present when your feet won't keep up? Every step is the very beginning of a leap.

Even when sitting, sit lightly as though just ready to rise. Learn for yourself. *Watch*. Don't let the past dog your heels.

Rhythm is the cycle with which moving things maintain their equilibrium. Rhythm is the pulsebeat of the melody of life and movement, and for the one who would learn to walk beyond the confines of the past, a valuable tool. But a tool that can't be wielded by a stiffened hand or mind. When you walk rhythm is the most important thing. Not speed but rhythm. If you would really know the art of walking you have to learn to enter a greater rhythm than that of thought. Every organism has its proper range of rhythm, and when you know how to let yourself slip effortlessly into that groove, into that greater rhythm, the pressures and jerks that distort the frame (and hence the mind) subside. The mind becomes quiet easily when you move beyond the splintered rhythm of thought. Learn to walk in such a way that the mind becomes quiet, deep, and observant. Walk onward in the pulse of a greater rhythm. That greater rhythm, beyond the contractions of thought, cannot be learned but rather entered. If you attempt to carry it with you it immediately becomes awkward and unwieldy. If you reduce it to technique you'll be left grasping at fragments a hairsbreadth away from expansiveness. It is a *sense* of rhythm that's enriching. A sense of rhythm that allows the body to move with graceful agility. It is to sense that rhythm in which the organism functions most smoothly, most naturally, at any given time as in the natural gait of the healthy animal. To *sense* that rhythm is to be transformed for it is a sensitivity beyond technique. An intent *listening* to a beat beyond the twitching of thought. Feel what it is to sense that flowing rhythm where the mind is not pressured, whipped by its own compulsion, and the mind effortlessly regains its vast silence. Walk as a wayfarer whose journey continually unfolds within the living present. A journey on which everything you see or hear, every arising and falling away, is not apart from something which is not apart from you.

Learn for yourself. *A teacher can't help you here.* Watch. But first ask yourself why you need to be told. Why you have allowed yourself to stop learning about those things most basic to your life. If you attempt to learn without asking those questions, you can never pass beyond technique. You'll only trap yourself again and again, a skin's thickness away from the living present. Caught one step behind the arisings, which have already changed as you stretch out your hand in greeting.

Clouds began to form but they were the type that enhance by complementing rather than obscuring the mountains. Billowing, pure white cumulus clouds that changed shape with each passing moment smoothly, not by fits and starts. Continually, a grand visual symphony played, swirling above the snowy mountain peaks. The woods began to thin as dark firs gave way to sparser lodgepole pines. Everything opened up gradually, and you found yourself standing on a huge level meadow with a broad white peak directly ahead. The air had grown progressively warmer under the rising yellow sun. Snow still lay in large softly sculpted mounds scattered ingenuously around the meadow. An artist would not have let them lie the way they were but here they lay, echoes of the mountain that lay ahead.

Tiny gems of frost clung to each blade of grass that remained in the shadows of small stands of pine trees. River willows, newly soft green and vaguely round, lined the lush banks of a meandering alpine stream. Polished stones, whose sharp edges had long since worn away under the insistent shaping of the flowing stream, lined the flat bottom, their round upper surfaces magnified by the absolutely clear, cold water. A red-tailed hawk and an enormous raven swung in leisurely interlocking circles in front of the blanketed mountain under the swelling, ever-changing clouds. Small songbirds sang faintly but sweetly in the pines under the powder blue sky.

You walked up the bank of the crystalline clear stream, toward the mountain. Your knees are flexible and your steps light and quiet so as not to jar things around. If you jar things around you move slower with more effort, more strain, and your mind becomes jumpy instead of broad and expansive like the mountains just ahead. Your mind loses its ease and becomes compressed by narrowing bands of thought.

Animals may run or walk, may lope and bound; they might spring or pounce, but they never jog. Only people jog, people who have read books. So they jar their frames, compacting them into submission, and compress their minds. Walk or run, each step a leap into the present, each footfall a light, soft landing with no thought to remain there. Sit that way too, not slumped but in the first increment of rising to your feet. Comfortably ready rather than feeling like a victim of gravity or looking like a pawn of inertia. Steer with your head, let it be light, buoyant. Relax your knees. Sense the greater rhythm and enter it, the rhythm that determines an infant's breathing, your heartbeat when asleep. Let the mind become large and quiet. Sense the rhythm and come to sense *timing*, the art of being moved at the correct moment.

The mountain was in the stream, both on the surface and in the glittering white of the polished stones in the streambed. Reflecting easily despite the rapid flow of the current. You looked up and its snowy white mass seemed to have doubled in size. You had to turn your head now to see it all. It was the purest white you had ever seen and it floated in the blue sky. The day was incredibly fresh and clear and you walked in it, step by step, each step complete in and of itself. Each step the beginning of a leap into the infinite present. The mountain enfolded you, and though you didn't look back you listened back to hear the raven yelling in the meadow.

The mind is stopped, stunned and still, and you walk through the silence toward the mountain, each step a leap into the deep silence, which is always present, always unfolding, always mutely offering its giant hand.

ISLANDS

THERE WAS A HUGE snowfield right beneath the glaciers, and it was like a rolling white sea flowing out from the mountain; a grand ocean that seemed fed by the thick white lakes and thin fingers of rivers, which hung suspended almost vertically on the mountain face itself. You could tell it was early to be so high because the pasque-flowers were in bloom at the edge of the sea; they only bloom here at timberline as the first snows begin to melt. The purity of their creamy petals added another dimension of white to a brightness in which everything was bathed, a brightness that was a much greater ocean than this homogeneous snowy sea.

You walked across the rolling waves and the spring snow crunched agreeably with each step. A raven flew by softly cawing with every beat of its large wings, as if mumbling something important under its breath. It called absently while otherwise engaged, in the way someone might hum while busily at work. There were nutcrackers bouncing everywhere, and their voices were the more incisive.

The raven flew over a crystal stream that passed beneath the snow and then flew straight at the mountain peak. It was big and knew it and flew by like a relic of some prehistoric age. You could hear the stream flowing under the snow, and it had a bright sound, as if infused with the dazzling sea of reflected light. The sun shone overhead as if a small, round piece of the white ocean had broken away and floated up into the sky. Diamond white against a deep blue in which were interspersed fine, angel-hair wisps of a softer white. An underlying harmony of white passed through and tied each element of the scene together.

The raven's languid call echoed off the sheer rock ahead; the echo held an almost visual thickness. Scattered among the waves of frozen foam were domed islands and vessels, which sprung from and navigated the great sea of snow. Waves of white like frosting lapped up on the shores of the island and swelled the hulls of the dark ships. The mountain winds had formed ripples which seemed to be in constant serpentine motion if you didn't look at them too sharply.

The islands were atolls of whitebark pines; they were beautifully grotesque, twisted by innumerable driving winds, gnarled with jagged, broken tops and coiled limbs by the heavy snowfall of winter. White-barked pines, another shade of white in the scene. Only when you see a really old one does the name become apt. The thick trunks, a fine pattern of countless small, greyish-white scales. They seemed nobly clothed in soft, pale shrouds. The biggest of them wasn't really large, but they were quite old, and they stood like guardians of the islands. They stood on the smaller ships like wizened masts with dark sails. The ships, borne on the painted, static ripples, continually prowled the snowy inland sea.

There were other mountains standing grandly farther down the shore. They too were mantled with white, like the snow sea and the sun and the mottled white bark. The islands and ships stood as small worlds complete unto themselves. Islands of knowledge that struggled for an apparent autonomy, not realizing the identical nature of all the activity on each. They were kinged and captained by authoritative sounding nutcrackers, brassy and bold as any pirate or monarch might be. They also formed the bulk of the noisy populace and the raucous crew of each. Once in a while they changed ships, winging against the radiant blue sky, a flash of white beneath the tail.

The wind came in waves, a big strong gust each minute or so; then a quiet broken by the jaylike screams of the nutcrackers and the sweet counterpoint melody of small warblers, glinting with yellow. Those in-between calms of the wind held a soft whisper of the five-needled pines, which in turn held the clean, soft hum of your own nervous system.

If you're not ever quiet enough to hear that hum inside, your life will lack depth. There will only be the depth of a facade.

When you became quiet, the calling of the birds seemed to originate within you, not within your body, but within something else that suddenly partakes of you. The birds were held in it also; in something not entirely theirs, or yours . . . A chipmunk scurried out on the wide sea between the ship islands. It held something in its mouth, and it looked like an ant lost out on the snow. The trees on the islands were thick, and their branches interlaced, forming an intricate woven screen. The nutcracker scolded and laughed. You were on the edge of a cove as the mountain enclosed you with two long arms coming off of two great shoulders. The arms were just beginning to wrap around you in some primal embrace.

The stream sounded somehow like delicate glass chimes beneath the snow; there was an immense wedge of rock, a sheer cliff of striated reds and browns, running between the vertical lakes and rivers of snow that hung precariously on the face. The shadows at the edge of the wedge held a deep black that the eyes could not penetrate.

When your mind became really quiet and beheld the clean hum of yourself, that blackness, like the unseeable space behind your eyes, was held and bathed in the same bright something that held you and the birds, the mountains and seas along with everything else.

THE MEADOW

THE WALL OF SNOW collapsed and the resulting avalanche sent a rumbling jolt through the entire meadow. It seemed to vibrate for one long, suspended moment, softening the clarity of the scene, and then everything snapped back sharply into focus again, like a loosed rubber band. It felt like a sonic boom. Then there was an echo, but it sounded far away, did not knock the scene out of focus like the original shock.

You walk in and out of places and you never let them follow you in either direction, so each moment, every place, remains unpolluted by the past. You've traded time for a still freshness, and it's a fair trade. You offer up the ghost of the past and for that you get the life of the present. There's nothing else that you can have or want; life moves on like a meandering river, continually flowing toward an ocean that is always silently present, if and when you re-member to look. If you remember to remember.

The early morning light revealed a thick blanket of new snow, which had all but filled the deep cirques and set a generous dusting on the exposed ridges and walls. It looked like powdered sugar strewn from above by some giant hand. No matter how many times the summer snow might fall, it was always like something you had never seen before, and the whole world seemed bathed in a freshness that emanated from the wilderness like a fragrance.

The sky was less a sky blue than the radiant blue of a mountain lake that had somehow been suspended above. It was a blue you rarely see, even up high in the mountains.

The meadow was just opening up. Thousands of violets and creamy globeflowers sprang out of the new grass and adorned the round green banks of the alpine stream that meandered through the present, coursed and turned widely, every rock and pebble visible in the crystal water, wandering through the meadow that looked like a giant park. It was like a beautiful city park in the early spring, where the people had all vanished and grand showy mountains had appeared as if in exchange—another fair trade. It was a huge meadow to be so high, and yesterday's snow stood in thick, random clumps with a new dusting of white powder on top of them. White on white, like snow falling on a mirror, reflector and reflection joined.

Two mountain chickadees with black hoods flew back and forth in a strange up-and-down flight like outsized bumblebees. They were dancing the rites of spring. They didn't sing, but click-chirped with anticipation. A hawk turned lazy circles from above, surveying the scene. Two ravens cursed at it heartily from down below.

The water was like liquid ice and it coursed down only moments gone from its source, flowing down and away from the snow-filled cirques and hollows, like thoughts that you let escape with your breath. You let them escape so they don't destroy the freshness.

There was new hellebore tucked away in the corners near the trees. It hadn't unfurled yet, and looked like so many green fingers pushing persistently out of the damp earth. A deer looked out from behind the trees, her doe eyes an odd blend of patience and wariness, like a waitress at an all-night spot where trouble can erupt suddenly and often. A small pool stood in the cool shade, in a thick grove of firs covered over like a display case with a delicately thin and perfectly clear sheet of ice. It was puckered with fine lines that looked like scar tissue, as it if had broken and healed imperfectly. The water emptied out from under the glass ice at one end of the pool and trickled musically down into a hidden valley. It made a soft sound as if a thousand pitchers of various sizes were being poured in unison. Your eyes followed the sound down the hidden valley, and you listened with an ear that seemed at first to be lodged in your heart. Soon you heard the trickling chorus with every pore of your body. It somehow seeped into your pores and cleansed you from inside out. It dissolved everything on the inside except for an alert fullness, a fullness that everyone searches for.

The doe turned then, looked back once more in parting and vanished, moving with the trickling water down into the hidden valley. The two freshly clothed mountains stood both ahead of and within you and beckoned, calling in both directions at once. The new blanket made them appear to grow larger as you watched. The air was so clear that you could see every crevice and, it seemed, each small stone on every ridge. They beckoned from both within and without and created an impasse, an impasse in which everything stopped; everything, that is, except the chorus of the trickling water. And you let everything return to what it had always been, before your mind interfered.

When you looked through the grass, the golden alpine buttercups seemed to grow like flowering shrubs, high on the white mountains. A porcupine lumbered down the bank, and two kinglets sported on the far bank of the crystal stream. The sun was almost overhead, and the sky became a depth of blue as if a series of deep blue skies stood endlessly, one behind the other. The reflection of the shimmering white mountains stood guard at each bend of the meandering stream.

THE BLIZZARD

THE AIR CHANGED and the woods became submerged in a kind of eerie half-light as the blizzard approached. The steady crunch of snowshoes biting through frozen crust mixed and married with the creaking sound of tall straight pines and conical silver firs swaying in the chilling west wind. Up here, the west wind is the storm wind. Thin shreds of cloud wafted across the snow, floating by, silently wraithlike. Ghosts with no fixed abode, they wandered through the forest. The sky, where it could be seen through the dense cover of branches, was a nearly homogeneous swirling grey on grey. A snow-sky preparing to open shop.

The day had dawned clear with hardly a cloud, and the mountains, already covered with several feet of snow, stood out sharply, invitingly, just beyond the boundary of your thoughts. They stood huge and white and aloof. They seemed to be withholding something when you gazed at them from down below. Something they hinted at fulfilling if you would only come closer, become intimate with them. Drop your thoughts and become aloof with the mountains. Everything delivers because nowhere is anything withheld. Everything comes across when *you* come across. It's a matter of knowing how to get close; of learning to erase the gap by softening your own borders.

The sky was softening like that now, becoming thicker and lower. Shreds of fog within the trees became empty holes within the fog. Spaces in which to see and move; soft-walled moving chambers that floated silently through the forest, borne on sharp winds. Every detail of the fir's silvery bark looked sharp and distinct within the floating rooms of half-light that wandered noiselessly over the mountain. The wind suddenly cracked its whip and trees creaked louder and higher in pitch. The snowshoes crunched and squeaked as they compacted the bottom inch of snow in their tracks. The trees and snowshoes creaked together now in the same key as the wind howled through the winter forest. A solitary grey jay flashed through a clear patch in the fog. It screamed twice in a bizarre timbre as if part of the trio and then completely vanished as if swallowed up. It had flashed briefly through one of the many moving rooms within the cloud cover, existing for you for one long second as it traversed the ten feet of visibility between two indistinct walls.

It was past time to be back now and there was still a good distance yet to travel as the laden cloud dropped its waving tentacles around the mountain. The peak, once white and majestic in the sun, became cloud-hidden now, enveloped by the blizzard. The snow began falling through the trees and each flake rang on impact with the frozen crust like countless infinitesimal pieces of broken crystal. Soon the odd tracks that steadily followed you would vanish under the freshly fallen snow.

A squirrel scolded you from a low branch, its voice harsh and insistent against the faultless harmony of wind-swept evergreens and crunching snowshoes. The sense of urgency in its voice reminded you to move on and not tarry; to leave the maze of deep woods behind, with its soft padded rooms of wet clouds and deep snow, and find the trail that would take you home again. The trail that you could follow by feel, whether the visibility was good or not, because it was the same trail that took you in. The same trail that you left when you entered the trailless deep woods.

Hours earlier you traversed the forest and came to a steep rise, plowing straight up, sweating, stamping imprints in the hard snow under a pale blue sky. There you saw the five snow-covered peaks around you and they appeared as close as thick fingers on a white-gloved hand that was your own.

And you stayed there, watching, letting the mountains act on you, cleansing you of viewpoints and other unnecessary things. Extra things. Let them wash you clean with their white expansiveness. You were washed clean by softening your borders and remembering the substance you both shared. You became aloof, cool like the mountains around you, but only aloof to thoughts of being unique. Of living out a life isolated from the whole. Ceasing to be unique you become expansive. Becoming ordinary again, you become majestic.

The storm was coming in then. Thick grey clouds were backed up on the western side of the mountains, waiting, brewing, gathering forces for a grey crossing into the sea of pale blue.

So while the sun still shone you sat on a deadfall and stayed, watching the storm come in. You watched and listened, and though you didn't concentrate on your breathing, you were aware of it anyway. Although you didn't hold to the expansiveness you felt it anyway. *The mind that perceives without effort is your only real treasure.* Through that effortless seeing, all phenomena are transformed into gems. You come to it easily like returning home at the end of a long day.

The clouds finally moved through the gaps and then regrouped. They began to look like an advancing grey tidal wave. A wave that would inundate everything in its path with a falling sea of new snow.

So you backtracked through the woods and with each crunching footfall moved closer to the way home. Through the shreds of damp cloud and through the floating chambers of clarity in the fog. The way was easy to follow in the new flakes of snow that had just begun to fall. Backtracking is the way to that expansive mind that is indifferent to its own life story. Backtrack to remember the treasure of your effortless perception. Fold back on yourself. Backtrack. Just follow the thread of any thought, any breath, any perception at all back home. *It's not far.* Go back the way you came and you're instantly there. All roads lead away from Rome. *You'd better turn around.*

Everything, even the snow-covered branches and laden clouds, each particle of ringing snow, was held lightly, easily, within the expansive mind. The snow fell harder now and it was becoming difficult to see, but the trail back was easy to follow; backtracking, you felt more than saw your way and soon there it was next to the huge old pine. The final bend.

THE CROSSROADS
OF WILLINGNESS

THERE WAS A WOMAN down in the village where you bought gas, and her eyes were flat like dull coins, as if she had sold off the last thing of value from her life in some moment of desperation, and then finally, after years, resigned herself to its loss.

Of course there *had* been a loss, many of them, each on the heels of the last, but what she really missed was probably not the thing that she thought that she had lost; it was more akin to a feeling of homesickness for a somewhere that she had never been. She looked at you appraisingly, but when eyes are dull, they can only see the surface of things, and her glance didn't penetrate, but only bounced off the outermost layer. There are a lot of eyes like that running around.

It was good to re-enter the wilderness, it felt like a much-needed shower. A deer froze in a clearing, watching you intently, every muscle poised and ready. A striped squirrel clung to the end of a broken branch, scolding sharply. The doe bounded off into the thick woods, and a dark blue Steller's jay flew by, low to the ground from the very space, the same doorway into which she'd vanished. Their eyes were lively, they all sparkled with life. When their eyes become flat, like dull coins, it means they are dying or already dead. When you let your eyes become dull like that, you too begin to die. What takes days or hours in the wilderness may take years in the village or in the city; technology is our life-support system, and it can keep the dying ones alive for a long time. It takes the place of a healthy alertness. Slow death takes its toll. In the village, there is something very common that is very rare in the wilderness—death by terminal complacency. Long-term decay, as opposed to the sudden end of the swift claw. It is the death of choice nowadays, death by complacency. The world and oneself unexamined, taken for granted. A world not worth watching. Most become caught, early in their days, and then live out a life of sheer flatness, which is only possible in this era of technology.

The clouds were moving in from the southwest, piling up in thick banks against the far side of the mountain like thick, sheared wool. This side of the sky was deep blue, but hazy as if there were a fire somewhere down the range. The mountains are a little snowier again this week; the snow pattern is always changing, moving endlessly up and down the steep slopes. Of course, the snow that appears to move up and down is never the same snow, it's always moving, combining, melting, changing, and the one who watches the snow that appears to move is never the same one either—that one too is like the snow, moving and combining, melting and changing, both in a state of blessed flux; both only the flux itself.

Where then is there room for complacency, for having flat eyes and dying of terminal dullness? Why so willing to let the profound erode into the mundane? The depth of the moment is continually alive with a keen sharpness, which dull eyes transform into a kind of living mush. If you live in that mush, your eyes will never penetrate anything, they'll just bounce right off the surface of everything. You become willingly trapped in a status quo of your own making. Of course it's because you become *willingly* trapped that you're so hard to rescue.

There was the undertonal sound of unseen flowing

water, and there were birds singing and chasing and pairing off and disappearing. A first wisp of thick cloud, like the vanguard of an approaching storm, found a chink in the mountain's armor and floated on through unaccosted. Soon the sky above became a homogeneous grey and a soft, crashing thunder rolled off through the forest, vibrating through each tree and stone. A bullfrog croaked loudly, sharper than the soft, faraway thunder. The birds all had glittering eyes, which flashed and sparkled even in the greyness, almost as if they had shone by themselves rather than the reflected afternoon light. The sky overhead became cleaved into two great hemispheres by a sharp line of equator; one was hazy blue, the other a swirling, wispy grey like old cotton.

Don't be so willing to get yourself trapped; become willing to see your own complacency. It's not a good thing to die of. Rouse your mind until your status quo dissolves; emit some light from your eyes, just enough to dissolve the dullness and no more—that's a good start. Let things return to an unforced state. Look at things in such a way that your eyes don't bounce off surfaces. Leave the overdeveloped and return to the wilderness of your mind, bathe there, rest there a while.

A soft green rain began falling in the pines; a crystal drop clung to a soft needle like a lustrous pearl and the wind was like a gentle caress. Suddenly the forest was soaked in the fresh mustiness of rich, damp earth.

THE FLOW
AND THE DREAM

THE SKY FROM HORIZON to horizon was a robin's-egg blue, and the afternoon had become almost hot under the brilliant rays of the spring sun.

The high snow on the mountains was melting fast, cascading down in clear, cold torrents, which swelled a thousand streams below and filled the lakes nearly to flooding. The topmost edge of the high water moved swiftly down the ancient streambeds, past the tall, straight pines, which formed an inviting grove of intimate shaded avenues. One stood like a king, taller and straighter, dwarfing the others. The sun was yellow, hot and bright on the very border of the refreshing coolness of the dark shade. It was the long, unending sound of flowing water that roared and trickled and rang like the bright ringing of a thousand celestial bells. The huge old pine that stood on the bank of the archetypally beautiful mountain stream had stood there long before the coming of the others, had stood continually immersed in the sonorous resonance of the singing water. Not a thin sound, but a rich composition of many inseparable layers like the parts of a chorus, which had blended into a single, primal song, astonishing for its ever-arising freshness. A rare music, which through its very continuity evoked still silence, *was* that silence, or at least void of concept, of artifice—if, that is, the little mind did not smother everything; if you remembered to listen.

The branches of the long-needled pine spoke a willowy language today as they swayed gracefully in the light warm breeze. The ancestors of its needles had been swaying, dancing with other winds, older winds, for hundreds of years, ever cleansed, ever renewed, by the fresh winds that blew off the mountains. Even the summits would melt off today, but soon would come other storms, those occasional storms of late spring. It could snow at any time of year up here and often did, even in midsummer. Then the streams would swell again and the fresh white blanket would melt away again under the heat of the yellow sun. Pass on, everything passing except the silent music that continually emerged as an undertone in the chorus, changing and yet not changing from one moment to the next.

A group of flycatchers with yellow throats suddenly materialized, all of them alighting in one brief instant in a small clump of elderly wizened junipers. A thick cloud of insects hovered over the rolling waters, each moving furiously, and yet the grey cloud just hung motionless, suspended over the lush streambed. Abruptly, as if seized by the moment, each of the small birds, one by one, darted from its perch into the swarm and then, just as abruptly, seemed to return to the same spot on the very same branch. They decorated the soft grey-green of the junipers like moving, living ornaments. Everything, even the cluster of mountains, was immersed in the sound of the rushing water.

The snowy peaks stood like sharp, clear thoughts far at the end of the descending stream, and yet they seemed so close, felt so close, as if your shoulder might brush the thick covering of snow if you turned too quickly or too carelessly. The grey cloud of insects, moving as one and following some unknown impulse, flew off downstream, away from the melting snows. They seemed to be supported by the resonance, they moved *through* it, within it, as fish swim through water. The flycatchers also moved as one, flitting down the stream. Their wings seemed supported by the roar that emanated from the water, as much as by the air. They didn't hesitate for a moment, but darted from their perches immediately, yellow throats flashing against the junipers and robin's-egg sky.

They had no attachment to what had been; they lived only as the unfolding present. Their vacated perches vanished behind them without a thought and new ones, fresh and promising perches, materialized ahead just in time for a new landing. The junipers did not look at all bare now without their ornaments. They were clothed in that primal sound with the ancient pine and the mountains with their melting snow.

There are some who are always carried away by the current, and they become blind to the flow. Carried away, they seldom hear the underlying celestial music, feel the beatless rhythm of its flow. They suffer because they are caught by the current and so must live out the linear stream of time, a life within a narrow stream of events, like living in an endless tunnel. A dimension has become lost somewhere and everything has become flat.

But there are others—others who can lose their self-importance in the depths of the resonance only to re-emerge as the present. They dive in and join the tall trees and the snowy mountains. They join and they move through that underlying harmony like fish swimming in water. Though the current of life may take its abrupt turns and sharply plummeting cascades, the resonance easily, timelessly, accompanies the moving water and then there is no attachment to the transient, to that which is always vanishing behind. There is no longer any confusion about getting somewhere; there's only the deep, eloquent resonance, the depth of the present that has swallowed everything. And it's always there for those who look, who know how to listen timelessly, adding nothing.

The grand old pine stood serenely, immersed in that celestial music, moment by moment steady, a stalwart guardian of the endless stream that nurtured it. Strong and solid, unmoving at the thick base, its long, soft needles swaying gently as feathers in warm wind. Alive it was, and unfolding as the present, retaining only the flow, nothing more.

THE SKY BEHIND
THE CLOUDS

THE THUNDER HAD FLOATED on the wind for hours and
the world above was still blue in patches sewn on a dark
grey sky. Two mountain bluebirds fell out of the grey,
spiraling down amorously around each other, descending
like paired keys of a falling samara in the wind.

Although only midday, it had gradually grown dark as
dusk and the air had become still and thick. Still and thick,
yet somehow porous at the same time with large holes like
empty spaces, invisible yet palpable spaces that allowed
the sweet smell of new grass to waft up into the lowered
pressure. Some say that they can smell the coming rain,
but what they really smell are the smells that have been
pressed into the earth and then released. They rise up like
balloons when the atmospheric pressure falls.

The crickets began to sing slower and slower, then
paused between their songs until finally hushed by the
dark promise of the coming storm and became silent altogether. The bluebirds playing love games earlier vanished
back into the grey. The brilliant male especially looked
like another small blue patch on the grey sky. They finally
alighted on a branch, softly nuzzled and touched beaks,
then flew off together somewhere. They disappeared only
moments after the crickets had begun their silent vigil.

The thunder advanced almost ponderously, lumbering
nearer with every grumbling crash. Becoming gradually

louder, enduring longer, yet somehow sharper than before. It was brewing and building all morning. Each crash rang out of the emptiness suddenly and then was gone like the cricket songs and the amorous bluebirds. Like every bit of moving phenomena inside or outside your mind. Each crash was a thought that arose and passed away, easy to perceive, impossible to hold in place.

The empty spaces in the air became hollows filled with a dormant electricity that was charged with a potential energy made up of countless microscopic flashes of lightning. Rain began to fall as if hurled down from above. It was mixed with hard pellets of hail. Lightning flashed brilliantly only yards away, just half an eyeblink ahead of the powerful thunderclap. The impact of the bolt moved effortlessly through your skin border, vibrating on silently through you for a sparkling moment like an echo that was caught within your body in the aftermath. It had crashed clear through you and then was still again like just one solitary beat of a mountain-sized heart.

Two distant patches of blue floated on the horizon, looking like small bright eyes on the faraway head of an enormous grey reptile. The blue eyes faded and became vacant in the timeless moment of the brilliant flash. They were washed out for one instant, one thought-moment, and then they refocused, blue and small and bright again as if regaining consciousness, intently watching once again the wild play of the black storm. The watcher forgetting everything for one brief moment. Forgetting even the watcher too, but not the arising and falling away of each distant crash, of every cloud movement comprising its very own body. The clarity of the blue eyes is a potent vacancy. They're the glimpsing glimpses of the unconditioned peeking through the raging storms of life. The emptiness that allows all things to arise and fade. *They're your very own eyes.*

The lightning arose and departed with abrupt swiftness, always leaving a slate-grey sky like a blank screen. A movie of a grey sky covering the blue sky behind. A grey screen pincushioned by countless needles of driving rain.

Each thought is like the lightning, instantly arising and departing, never staying. Each thought is also like the portentous hollows in the air. Hollows completely full of countless small flashes of lightning. The content of those hollows is unconditioned energy—you can see that, appreciate the still power of the potential energy of your mind, the blue sky of your being, if you let all the thoughts arise and depart swiftly like lightning. Do you notice the lightning more, or less, for its brevity? Most know only the kinetic energy, the arisings, and try to exist within a status quo without departures, caught within the swirling mass of grey clouds that only mask the clear blue eyes of watchfulness.

A cold norther begins to howl and a tumbleweed catapults past. The wind howls for one long moment and then fades. The two eyes of blue on the horizon are combining into one large round hole like the vacant orbit of a cyclops. A shaft of light suddenly bursts through the grey and it instantly becomes day again. A blue window opens directly overhead. The blue has never left, for it has passively watched the entire play of dark clouds from up above. The grey clouds are becoming whiter now, turning and combining, twisting like towels and breaking apart like china. The torrential rain has become a light spring shower. The sky holds it all easily, without complaint, without comment.

Know your mind as the sky; allow everything to pass on through, the clouds, the lightning, the winds, all of it, even the blue itself. *Don't even get caught on the blue*. For it can be seen but never grasped. Find the underlying, the screen on which it is all projected; constantly look for the projector. See and hear whatever arises, but don't grasp at anything. *Don't even get caught on the sky.*

The air was washed clear and clean after the storm. It seemed to tingle with a lively current as if each particle in the air were quietly singing. A rainbow appeared in the east. The sky was completely blue overhead. A frog began to croak sonorously. The pair of bluebirds reappeared with the sun. He was deep blue, almost turquoise like the sky. She was smaller and lighter in color. He tried to perch next to her, but she eluded him playfully. Then he chased her toward the mountains, off into the dazzling yellow afternoon sun.

THE PANORAMA

STOP AND LOOK AROUND YOU. Look out from the frameless window of a long pause and let images come to you rather than chasing outward after them. Allow yourself to reorient so that you're no longer pulled along by the stream of events. For if you would *see* differently you'll have to learn to *look* differently. Let the subtle inner tensions dissolve, those unnoticed strivings that you've become used to looking through. Stop looking out through tense eyes on a pinched face. Those are the frames in your conceptual windows. Let all that go. Do it easily like letting your breath go with a sigh. Become still inwardly and let the innumerable images of change come to you. Don't mind letting them surround you all at once. Don't be afraid to let them move through you, fill you momentarily and then depart without friction, only to be followed by the endless parade of others. Let them all go. When you finally become willing to let them move at their own pace, the panorama that contains them all will fill you. Stop and look around innocently as though for the very first time. A fresh first time devoid of other times and other places.

The rain stopped and the mountaintop was clothed in a dark, damp chill. Shreds of cloud moved silently through the depths of the night. The long, drumming rain had stopped and vanished silently into the darkness. It left behind a void, which was immediately filled by other sounds, by the whistling of the wind in ancient firs and the pounding of elk hooves in the nearby meadow. By something small and scurrying, which was performing an invisible repetitive action in the dark. Three days of continual drumming rain departed and left a residual roar that quietly and insistently continued to work within your body like a soft vibration. It felt like a fine pattering of echoes.

It's easy to become linear in scope and to lose your depth by the wayside. When you make your home within the shallows, becoming lost in the flattened world of thought, your vision narrows accordingly. Literally. If you live from knot to knot on an endlessly knotted string, your vision narrows to sight down that interminable clothesline. Visual functioning actually narrows in scope to accord with the world in which you have come to believe; a land of gettings, a long succession of knots, a complex collage of inner tensions through which to look. Small windows with tinted glass. A convenience world in which to shop your life away, acquiring things that you don't really need. *Is that enough?*

The drops of rain had become a mist of fine droplets that enveloped everything. It even filled the spaces between each finger. Though the rain had stopped, the cold black pearls were thrown in false downpours off the branches of hoary old firs. Cyclically the wind would ebb and then begin to blow and then a spray of heavy drops would whip the black duff beneath the shadowy trees in the cold invisible mist.

When life becomes reduced to a series of gettings, to mere knots tied on a long string, whole dimensions become lost as the world becomes compressed to accord with your limited needs. The world begins to look just as narrow as that which you want from it. Those dimensions become lost somewhere, and the remainder is a world utterly without depth—and without richness, for the *rich-*

ness of the world fades along with those lost dimensions of depth. What's left is just a narrow corridor of successive events, a flat filmstrip of images. Your own personal domino theory in action. *Is that enough for you?* To live imprisoned in the shallows is to live estranged from the fathomless depths of richness. To lose the vision of the panorama is to live with a sense of loss, a recurring hollowness.

The rain had stopped abruptly as if a tap had been turned off, and now the first star in several nights appeared above. It glittered in a round blue-black hole, which was opening like a pupil in the iris of swirling clouds overhead. A fragment of cloud, a mote, was momentarily stranded within the hole, wispy arms radiating out centrifugally like a spiral nebula. The very edges of the clouds surrounding the dark hole and the wispy shreds of the nebula were softly illuminated by an unseen moon, which was still cloaked in a thick veil of clouds. For days the mountaintop had been totally immersed in the continually falling rain, enveloped by laden clouds that had descended on a bright afternoon. Now the clouds were clearing; the night sky peeked through and you felt yourself to be a dot surrounded by a full emptiness into which both you and the wispy cloud borders began to dissolve and vanish.

The brain easily adapts to life within the tunnel; easily adjusts down to an order of decreasing function. It readily conforms to the limited needs of a life lived within a shallow world constructed by thought, a life lived within a long hallway. Vision accommodates most helpfully to delete what isn't being used. For it is in the brain that sight takes place, the eye but a lens and photocell. When the brain adapts to accommodate to the limited motives of thought, the panorama in which we move literally vanishes and gives way to a world that can then be seen only sequentially. A world of successive points; a small world that merely drips on you rather than inundates you fully.

When the panorama vanishes the fathomless flow of life becomes like reading sentences across a page. One line at a time. A scenario *about* life, which can never escape the borders of the printed page. The result is a life that can never strain at its own format, only its syntax, because it lacks the wholeness of vision to see the page on which it's printed. An unexamined life results, which can no longer see its own limitations, no longer see the lack of depth inherent in that linear way of seeing. When we live within the limits of that scenario, scarcely bumping the edges, never pushing back the borders, vision actually changes to adapt to the loss and finally comes to see in no other way. *Is that enough?*

It was rare for a rainstorm to last so long up here. Mountain thunderstorms are more apt to be like brief affairs. Intense and finished. A release of pent-up energies and then a definite parting in which the sun once again has room to shine in the space between two people or two clouds. Or like spats between old friends. Terse and fierce and then over. It usually comes on like that, with little warning. An advancing island of cold, wet grey surrounded by unreachable sunshine and blue on every side. A statement that engulfs you with its meaning, a statement that once made quickly loses its force. Loses its impact and vanishes back into the whence from which it came.

Days before, the last visible sunrise had been a deep blood red. Now, a thin shell of the brilliant moon edged out from behind eclipsing, spent storm clouds. Its white light illuminated the winding curtains of phosphorescent vapor, which filled the immense foreground between you and the rugged pinnacles ahead and formed a bridge. A bridge of silver moonlight, the brightest light you'd seen in days. Several acres of softly rolling alpine meadowland were transformed into a moonlit park. A pair of mule deer eyes glowed in the thin mist like reflectors in a fog.

Suddenly the wind picked up and shiny black drops of rain were thrown down diagonally through the pale light. Deer browsed the edge of the meadow, their flanks emitting a soft glow into the night. Both you and the peak were swallowed up together by the silver light. Just two Jonahs blended together in the luminescent belly of the night. Immersed in a pool of light, blended together while yet remaining distinct. The mountain's face and your own both washed by the same night winds that tore the ever-widening blue-black hole in the clouds overhead.

Become aware of the compulsion that propels you through the tunnel. Become alive to the feeling of the carrots that pull you along the string of knots. Become aware and just expose it all to the silver light. Like a barometer, feel the internal pressure that stops the new from entering. Become awake to your own personal high-pressure system. A portable high-pressure system that not only protects you from the new, from the threat of change, but is easy to carry about. Keep your eye on it.

There exist four-dimensional beings who live and move omni-directionally within a multidimensional world. Yet those beings have come to look and see with tunnel vision by living out of a series of gettings; by moving along from knot to knot. Living like successive lines of prose and missing the forest for flat photographs of each successive tree. There are beings whose disordered vision cannot see the compulsion that propels them down the tunnel of becoming. Becoming this or that incessantly.

Occasionally an immense landscape appears, a conundrum that momentarily challenges the habitual functioning by its very immensity, by its ungraspability. But a new photograph is quickly ordered from the files, which is but an enlargement of the old picture; a photograph that blots out even more of the view while remaining just as flat.

The two-dimensional mind of flatness is one which *thinks* about awareness, which *thinks* about the vastness beyond thought; which seems to pause in the movement of compulsion but does so in order to *think* about the end of compulsion. Out of that false pause emerges a world of flatness, which is like looking at a painting or a movie. A series of images in which imagination postulates a more desirable future toward which to move and the compulsion of the one-dimensional mind will propel you there. So the interior pressure remains high and you live without discovering the pause into which something new can enter. The panorama has vanished, the world that can *fill* you is gone and vision functions narrowly, perfunctorily, limited in scope by the long hallway of habit. A flat world results in which it should be possible to sail off the edge into a limitless expanse, yet its boundaries are too closely protected by the walls of thought. Walls which are carefully guarded by the sentries of self-image.

The moon edged out from behind the filmy eclipse of clouds into the jagged opening, which was torn ever wider as the clouds dispersed. It slowly grew into a white gibbous moon, which cast a cool, pale sheen on the almost day-lit tops of tall black firs and on the softly glowing bowl-like glacier, which lay in the crux of the rugged spires ahead. The pinnacles stood like sentinels above the amphitheater surrounding the glacier. They were clad in flowing grey shrouds, which clung in wisps to the escarpment, magnetized and held by the cool bulk of the snowy rock.

The sky was growing lighter in the east. The deer had gone, nothing moved now as even the winds were swallowed by the pause before dawn. The pause wasn't forced but rather the natural space between two breaths. The inhalation of the night and the exhalation of the day. Then the dawn winds picked up—you could hear them rising far away, like the sound of a waterfall in a deep canyon. You could hear them approaching, moving through the trees, advancing, long before they actually arrived. With each increasing gradient of daylight the sky grew clearer of spent clouds and the peak became wholly tinted in a fiery pink alpenglow. The iron oxide towers, which were suspended by grasping fingers of snow, turned blood red in the glow of dawn. The wind was clearing the clouds and the sky became a pale blue sea on which pink shreds floated like vessels in the cool morning.

The long rain had eroded much of the snow that covered the meadow. Huge elk tracks crisscrossed the opening that surrounded a small craterlike pond. The earth seemed washed clean and the new grass looked fresh against the remaining mounds of snow. Knotweed pushed out from beneath the rapidly melting snow and looked crimson in the pink morning air.

The spaces between your thoughts are like scattered fresh springs emerging from your very depths. Those springs continually bubble up between the words and sentences of thought—anywhere there's a space at all—and indicate those deeps that lie beneath the linear world of thought. When the depth between thoughts, the depth of the still mind, merges with the depth of the world, the mind enters into its surroundings! *Enters* rather than *recognizes*. There is awareness but the sense of the linear has vanished. Then the mind can enter into its surroundings rather than merely living within a story it insists on telling. A story it compulsively feels it must finish. When the mind forgets the diminished world through taking part in its surroundings, vision becomes whole again. Becomes panoramic. Wide angle. And somehow fused to a sense of depth that bubbles up continually like a spring. There arises an awareness of the depth that fills the *volume* of the scene. A boundless depth radiating through and far beyond the movie screen of habitual vision.

When the mind knows how to let go of things with a mental sigh; when it reorients to the primacy of the bottomless springs that arise between every shallow thought rather than the content of the thoughts themselves, the knotted string dissolves, compulsion withers away and the world becomes multidimensional again. The way it *is*. Panoramic vision is restored as the brain relaxes its arbitrary borders and participates in its surroundings.

The amphitheater loomed ahead and seemed about to engulf you. It grew larger with every step. The air was vibrant; there was a palpable energy that filled the air as you approached. You moved in it and of it like a fish through water. It was not stopped by any visual borders but seemed to move through your body and the massif equally. An energy that both composed and encompassed you. There was a force in the air that almost crackled. Something that was not excitement, that didn't quicken the pulse and yet enlivened you totally. It was like walking beneath huge power transformers. It seemed to charge every cell, and the brain was alive and alert. The air became chilled as you advanced. A cool wall of air numbed your face as you met the cold breath that descended from the icy bowl.

The slope was steep and you had to climb by kicking steps into the rain-softened snow. Kicking your toes into the snowfield and walking up your own staircase. A torrent of water rushed beneath the snow from a small notch in the caldera. Its course was marked by lichen-encrusted boulders from whose exposed facets the snow had melted. The water rang musically in certain spots and roared in others. You skirted the boulders where you could and continued upward. The mountain became too large to see clearly now and the glacier vanished from view. You felt the mountain more than saw it as you moved closer. Your thoughts also become hard to see when you get too close to them. Like the mountain they become feelings when you begin to lose the distance. A nutcracker screamed sharply from down below. You went slowly and moved as if emerging from out of a long pause.

There was no compulsion to reach the top. When you can explore without compulsion you then become guided by interest, by love, and the knotted string dissolves. When you can climb without being compelled, you can turn around at any time with no disappointment. *Everywhere* is just fine. Then the quality of your life can take a truly different tone. Not before. Then vision becomes full and you become penetrated by the same depth that you see around you. Then even the mountain peaks and far-off clouds, the face of a friend, are no longer separated from you by a wall of becoming. Walls that can continue through time and become endless tunnels. The faraway peaks and clouds, the faces of others, are cleansed of arbitrary borders and become the depth through which you move.

Cleansed of barriers of thought, perception becomes instantaneous. Even what is far away becomes near in that perception. The flat world created by thought disintegrates when you don't become lost within it. Let it arise or not but don't lose yourself there. Then the sequentially experienced world gives way to admit the vital collage of the world of depth. The panorama. There is a melting of borders and everything near or far is allowed through the gate unmolested, allowed to come and go freely.

The notch was much larger than it had looked from down below, and it dwarfed you as you climbed through it and down into a grand, deep silver bowl, which surrounded you on all sides. A huge silver bowl of glacial ice ringed by massive ramparts of striated red rock. A refrigerated amphitheater sunken into the core of the mountain, ringed by snowy pinnacles beneath a circle of blue sky. An unceasing cascade poured from the edge of the glacial ice and became the roaring, singing subsnow creek that flowed from the notch and coursed unseen down the boulder-strewn slope to the new spring meadows below.

The late afternoon sun was blotted out by the spires of

the caldera. You were *in* the mountain, nestled within its core, rather than on it. It held you there inside like an uncompromising yet loving mother. There was no view to the outside save that of the blue sky and a random puff of cloud. The spires were dripping with a white icing of snow that cracked sharply as pieces broke away and slid down the red and gray walls. The temperature had dropped thirty degrees when you climbed through the notch. The edges of small crevasses were tinted a deep glacial blue. Boulders littered the ice where they had broken free from the steep walls. Lying on its side like a fallen monolith was a huge lichen-encrusted pinnacle, which had broken off the inside wall of the north face and come to rest in the bottom of the bowl. It lay like a fallen hero on a barren arctic plain and its scale was such that you shrank to the scale of an ant beside it.

Not only were you inside the mountain but also inside of a palpable fullness that filled the volume of the caldera. You felt immersed in the starkness that surrounded you. Immersed in an echo-creating emptiness that enclosed you and stretched from wall to wall. The sky fell into the open top of the mountain and held you intimately within it. Everything near and far was admitted. Not successively, a piece at a time, but rather your surroundings poured through you like water through a sieve in an almost cellular massage. When the mind releases its tenacious hold on the knotted string, it allows many things to occur at once. *The way they really do.* Suddenly there is more to see than the severely foreshortened perspective of the endless tunnel, and then the panorama enfolds you. You *ease* back into your surroundings like something coming back into focus, and you feel alive as you can be in no other way.

Let go of your hold on the knotted string by simply not owning any of the knots. Ease back into the spaces between your thoughts and enter into the depths of your own perception. Don't own whatever arises and your brain will reorganize by itself. Vision will become panoramic and the richness of life will return with those lost dimensions.

There was the sharp crack of a rock breaking out of the escarpment and falling down the snowy wall. It whirred as it rolled across the frozen floor of the glacier and finally came to a stop on its newly fractured side. It left a faint trail of reddish hyphens lingering on the snow. The pinnacles above turned a dark shade of maroon as a wandering cloud floated by and closed off the top of the caldera. The remaining blue of the sky turned off and on as it moved through. There was a shrill scream from above and a diffuse shadow seemed to pass directly through you as it floated across the silver floor. A hawk was flying in slow motion across the caldera, passing overhead from spire to spire in a timeless flight through the hanging wisps of swirling cloud.

BEFORE DAWN

IT WAS THE LAST hour of a frigid winter night and the world outside was clothed in a light covering of new snow. The hard-edged world of objects and opposites had disappeared once more as it does each night. The diverse world of thought had fallen back into you as you sat perfectly still, listening, within a silver ray of moonlight that shone through the open curtains and lay snugly against the flat floor, shining on you, abruptly blooming and then fading away in the pale, cool light.

A great horned owl had hooted its quizzical call of inquiry for hours in the tall long-needled pine outside. *Who?* A question to stop the mind in its tracks and let the pale moonlight shine through. Off in the distance another owl replied, a muted echo of the same inquiry. *Who?* A query that falls back into you. A query such that you fall back into yourself and become as still as the winter night through which the night sounds fly.

The mountain peaks are illumined in the moonlight, their white shrouds of snow softly glowing like an altar in the clear, cold night air. The snow on the ground looks translucent rather than reflective. Everything seems immersed in the silver light, everything submerged within a luminescent silver sea.

At night you need to be very alert, for the night is a time of subtle energies, of rounded feelings and textures rather than the hardened thought forms of the day. Textures that tint perception spatially, palpably, even more insidiously than thoughts alone. Feelings move the mind around in their own way, making the chest tighten subtly and causing the ability to watch and listen to vanish. You have to be very alert, very sensitive to the most delicate of pressures so as not to be influenced by the countless nights of an immeasurable past. Feelings, textures. Watch them and listen, but don't interact with them. *No dialogues.* Let them be and yet watch them in the way the silver moonlight illumines the snowy mountain peaks. Listen to them like the stillness of the night through which the night sounds continually move. Watch and listen, let them bloom for you and then fade away. Don't own them but don't neglect them either.

A pack of coyotes sang to the desert moon and their lonesome call passed through your very core. It felt like light passing through a transparency. Off in the distance a dog barked back at them angrily, monotonously, like the simple beat of a machine. The coyotes teased it into barking each time it finally tired. They howled in chorus like a prairie wind blowing through the eaves. There was a snorting nearby and the sound of hooves thudding dully into the snowy earth outside the window. The silver moonlight began to fade and gave way to the drab darkness before dawn.

If you're very alert upon awakening you can watch your whole world, the world of objects and opposites, return again each morning. Watch it reappear from your depths, recreating itself every day. But you have to be very alert, sensitive to even the slightest flicker, the most delicate tendril of thought. Blink once the eye of awareness and you'll miss it.

When you awaken don't move a muscle, lie perfectly still and just watch. See the world come back to you, come back *from* you. Watch it arise from your surface like mists off a morning lake. With every object that you recognize the world will recreate a piece of itself by association with those objects. Though you may try, you cannot stem its flow. The world *will* arise and the one who lives in that facade will arise with it. The world *will* arise, but can its borders be watched from out of stillness? Do you know how to be free in spite of your world? Or because of it?

Realize that nothing at all belongs to you. Not only material things but your thoughts, your emotions, your reactions. Nothing. No possessions. They *will* arise, but don't possess them. Let everything be just the way it is. Like a visit to a museum. Look closely but don't touch anything. Watch everything, but possess nothing. See the conditioned nature of all you call your own. See the nature of your daydreamed world by watching it arise in the morning like mists off an early morning lake.

There was a soft glimmer of light in the sky and everything had been tinted with a dark wash of grey. The mountains and the snow on the ground were an undefinable pastel. The wind began to whistle and then howled a desolate melody as the sun began to rise.

You stood at the window and the glass flexed against the howling wind. You watched the mountains lighten with each passing moment. When the world disappears all that is left is that which has been unhandled by thought. All that's left is that which thought may dream about but never begin to touch. Watch and listen. Feel. *But don't own anything.* Let the coyotes sing for you on moonlit nights and let the lonely melody of the dawn winds sing you awake in the morning. But don't move into it right away. Lie still for a bit. Watch it happen all over again each morning. But be free whether it's there or not. When it arises just remember to watch and inquire like the owls. *Who?*

The sun rose higher and the wind became still. The warm alpenglow on the mountains deepened. Everything seemed absolutely still. The snow-shrouded peaks glowed intensely pink in the dawn of a new morning.

EMBARKING

THE JOURNEY ON MIND Mountain is a very different kind of journey, yet one that anyone can take at any time. It is an unparalleled exploration, in which no photographs are taken, no journals necessary, no specimens collected. It is like other mountain journeys in the sense that one's burden becomes lighter with each passing day. Yet it is unique in that it entails looking for that elusive traveler who journeys, looking out from the midst of a pause. It is to fall into a lively state of noncompulsion and from there observe our surroundings both interior and exterior. It is to fall awake. Only when we see the limited scope of thought can we pass beyond.

And though you journey far on Mind Mountain, you need go nowhere at all, for the richness of Mind Mountain is omnipresent, hand-in-glove with you wherever you happen to be. It is a journey that begins in the vast land of noncompulsion and also ends up there. It is a unique journey, for we explore the vastness by stopping rather than going, pausing to break the endless chain of reactions so that at last we can stop to look around. To observe from the midst of a pause. A sightseeing journey in the most profound sense. To see the world afresh, as if for the first time.

There is a kind of exploration that transforms the mind. Yet one can be motivated in that exploration solely by a love of truth; only by a vital interest in seeing clearly just where in fact one actually is. A journey of exploration fueled by genuine interest rather than by the compulsion that characterizes the daily struggle to stem the tides of change and maintain the little status quo.

When one falls in love with exploring the truth beyond memory, the truth that *contains memory* yet radiates far beyond memory on every side, when one falls with *that* which we have only later defined, the world is then permeated by mystery, alive with depth. To the one who learns how to really explore, rather than merely redefine, life becomes transformed into an adventure worthy of the name. *There is a kind of exploration that transforms the mind.* There is a sense of the mystical based on the clarity of *seeing* that has the power to transmute the mundane back into the profound. It is the journey of a life that can shed its past like a chrysalis, again and again. To be reborn, not just once but continually. It is the journey of a life of inspiration.

Why will we explore like this? To see where we are! To see where "here" is. As lovers of truth, no reason could be more potent—to find out where we are now before compulsively rushing off to a somewhere else. A somewhere else that will accompany us wherever we go, clinging to us like a double image. And there's no escape by merely rushing away. Why take the journey at all? After all, Mind Mountain is vast and unconquerable. Journey so that a new order of human being can exist—a human being with new possibilities. *There is a kind of exploration that can transform the mind.*

Explore then and become sculpted by what you see. Let the explorer be acted on by the exploration. A life of continual renewal is possible if we cease being compelled down the tunnel. A life of freshness. Open wide the gates and let the world beyond memory flood in.

The intense blue of the sky encloses like an endlessly deep canopy that feels somehow closer than your scalp, seems to have found its way into the thin space between your throat and the clear sheet of mountain water that you swallow. It's that rarest of wildflower meadows enclosed in a great hidden room, whose sparkling gems in dozens of varieties seem to cover every square inch of the lush green canvas, an intensity that short-circuits the wires of memory and releases the mind into a vastness beyond the canyon walls.

It is a scene beyond description, with a depth no camera could possibly encompass and capture on flat sheets of film. It is a dense jungle of purple and white lupines, paintbrush of every shade of pink, scarlet and orange, countless symmetrically creamy cat's-ears. You are stunned and still enough to feel the brain's role in the exchange of color. You and the million flowers seem but parts of an organic rainbow springing from the ground beneath the layer of grass. Each blossom, every petal, your own feet and hands outlined by the rich green of the grass and brilliant blue of the afternoon sky. There are countless butterflies and bees fluttering and buzzing throughout the flowers. One of the butterflies is yellow and black and blue like the deep blue of the sky above. Hummingbirds move from paintbrush to paintbrush, attracted only to the deepest reds. The deer merely look up at you and then resume eating, all wariness gone as if dissolved by their long stay in this heaven. The big grey jays are fearless as ever, but not so aggressive as usual, as if tempered by the magic of the hidden land. Nowhere is there any fear, as if it has all evaporated in the openness of the unencumbered feeling that is prevalent everywhere. Deep-hued evening grosbeaks, strikingly adorned in amber, black, and white, fly from branch to branch unconcernedly. A falcon glides the length of a long meadow, hunting only yards above the thick waves of wildflowers.

If you allow yourself to get taken up by the vastness, the way one takes up a thread or the strain of a song, you'll come to see the arbitrary border of the skin line. If you let the unencumbered swell move easily past that line often enough, like the tides through the three-mile limit, then that vastness will come to call on you more and more often, until you can never quite forget about it. Then the beauty will enclose you, far after the last of the flowers have faded.

Mountain Dawn is a nonprofit educational organization founded by the author in order to assist interested individuals in recapturing lost depth and richness in their lives. In a totally individualized and eclectic approach emerging from years of exploration and teaching in the martial arts, meditation and wilderness awareness, the author is available at certain times to vitally interested individuals and groups as a resource rather than a teacher.

In the pristine setting of the spectacular San Juan Mountains, one explores and observes both oneself and the intensely beautiful surroundings, allowing the conditioned mind to become stunned and still enough to pause so that a new quality can arise within. It is the author's conviction that this quality can only be uncovered in each person rather than developed. Completely free of any rigid system or approach that fosters dependence, Mountain Dawn emphasizes involuntary meditation as the only real teacher.

For more information write:

Avant Press
P.O. Box 526
Fort Collins, Co. 80522

WWW - CAShmere COmpany . Com
1-800-707-1948